THE

MICROWAVE HANDBOOK

Jill McWilliam

OCTOPUS BOOKS

IN ASSOCIATION WITH BEJAM

Above: Old-fashioned treacle tart (page 64) with Custard sauce (page 59).
Front cover: Sweet and sour lamb (page 45) and Green beans with almonds (page 53).
Back cover: Wholemeal apple and orange flan (page 60).

NOTES
Standard spoon measurements are used in all recipes
1 tablespoon = one 15 ml spoon
1 teaspoon = one 5 ml spoon
All spoon measures are level.
All eggs are size 3 (standard) unless otherwise stated.
For all recipes, quantities are given in both metric and imperial measures.
Follow either set but not a mixture of both, as they are not interchangeable.

Introductory text by Carol Bowen
Recipes developed by Joy Langridge

Published by Octopus Books Limited,
59 Grosvenor Street, London W1

First published 1985
© Octopus Books 1985
ISBN 0 7064 2235 X

Reprinted 1988

Printed in Hong Kong

CONTENTS

INTRODUCTION

As a perfect companion to the freezer, my microwave cooker has justified the original modest investment many times over.

It defrosts and cooks quickly, re-heats superbly, creates less washing up, it is simple to clean ... but the major benefit is that it cooks food better than conventional cookers. Not everything, of course: one of the principal rules of learning to use a microwave is not to neglect the conventional cooker — which is still better for tenderizing cheap cuts of meat and for grilling best steak.

But the microwave wins hands down on everything else. It preserves the flavours of delicate foods such as poultry, fish and vegetables as well as retaining more of the all-important nutrients often otherwise lost in the cooking liquid. Adding fats or liquids is also not usually necessary as the food holds its own natural moisture making the most of its true succulence and texture.

Doubts and fears

Are microwaves safe? This question is probably more appropriately asked of a conventional cooker — few of us have escaped minor burns or worse, and they give constant cause for concern when used by children or the elderly. Microwaves stay cool during cooking and have had to meet stringent mechanical and electrical safety requirements. Had there ever been any real question as to the safety of microwave cookers they would never have been allowed to go on sale in this country. It must be realized that the microwave cooker is just a more direct way of cooking food using electrical power — instead of the energy being used to heat the inside of an oven or a cooking utensil, the electricity is transformed into microwave energy which generates heat directly within the food itself. This energy is only present while the cooker is in action and disappears instantly the power is switched off. The cooking that continues during 'standing time' is merely by conduction.

Does microwave cooking save on fuel bills?

The speed and efficiency of microwave cooking can make a significant contribution to keeping down fuel costs. The exact savings are difficult to assess, but it is possible to halve expenditure, depending on the type of foods cooked and the frequency of use. Compare the following energy consumption and cooking costs based on a unit of electricity charged at 5.59p per kwh:

4 chicken pieces

microwave	0.40 kwh	2.24p
conventional	1.14 kwh	6.38p

Wholemeal loaf

microwave	0.10 kwh	0.56p
conventional	0.91 kwh	5.09p

Rhubarb and ginger pudding
microwave	0.23 kwh	1.29p
conventional	0.63 kwh	3.53p

2 herrings
microwave	0.04 kwh	0.23p
conventional	0.21 kwh	1.18p

500ml/1 pint of custard
microwave	0.15 kwh	0.84p
conventional	0.20 kwh	1.12p

2 scrambled eggs
microwave	0.03 kwh	0.17p
conventional	0.08 kwh	0.45p

1kg/2lb Christmas pudding
microwave	0.20 kwh	1.71p
conventional	4.17 kwh	23.32p

225 g/8oz frozen peas
microwave	0.09 kwh	0.51p
conventional	0.23 kwh	1.29p

Friends often ask 'What do you find most useful about your microwave?' The major benefits, such as speed, economy and cleanliness, I now take for granted – it's the hundred and one little uses that still make the microwave exciting as well as invaluable, such as:

*Making a pot of fresh coffee which can then be reheated by the cup through the day.

*'Instant' scrambled eggs for breakfast with no messy pan to clean.

*Drying stale bread to make breadcrumbs which can then be stored in the freezer.

*Non-messy blanching when the garden harvest is upon us.

*Warming bread rolls to serve with soup and softening the butter to go with them!

*Producing fresh homemade cakes and scones for tea at the last minute.

*And last, but by no means least, with a selection of prepared meals and a choice of vegetables in the freezer and the microwave to do the cooking the family cannot complain when they have to fend for themselves.

Jan McWilliam

THINK
MICROWAVE

Whether you are an enthusiastic cook who enjoys creating new recipes; a reluctant cook who prefers to spend as little time as possible in the kitchen; or a family cook who often has to produce a variety of meals at differing times, the versatile microwave has a lot to offer.

There is nothing difficult about cooking in the microwave – it is simply a matter of THINKING MICROWAVE.

If you already own a microwave cooker you will know where to begin, but this book will also serve to refresh your memory about microwave techniques as well as providing some new, up-to-the-minute information. There is also a whole host of delicious quick and easy recipes for you to try.

If you have just bought a microwave cooker then why not start by placing a cup of instant coffee in the microwave and heating it on HIGH for 1½ minutes, pull up a chair, put aside any rumours you may have heard, and read on. Then judge for yourself the almost 'magical' delights of the microwave.

What is Microwave Energy?

The mechanics of microwave cooking are simple. Inside the microwave cooker is a magnetron vacuum tube. This converts ordinary household electrical energy into electromagnetic waves which move at high speed within the cooker as they are deflected off the metal walls of the cavity. These are not as powerful as infra-red rays, nor are they in any way harmful in normal circumstances.

Microwaves are absorbed by the molecules of moisture in food, causing them to vibrate rapidly, producing heat to cook the food. The molecules vibrate many thousands of times a second, producing a very intense heat – hence the speed of microwave cooking.

Microwaves can pass through glass, pottery, china, paper and most plastics so these materials make ideal cooking containers. As metals reflect microwaves, food *cannot* be cooked in foil, metallic containers, or dishes with a gold or silver decoration.

THE MICROWAVE COOKER

All cookers consist of a basic unit of a cabinet, magnetron, wave guide, wave stirrer, power supply, power cord and controls. Some have additional features such as an automatic defrosting system, variable power control, browning element, turntable, or integral thermometer or probe, but the basics upon which all microwave cookers work remain the same.

Microwave energy is passed through a wave guide and stirrer into the cooker cavity. The cooker cavity deflects the microwaves from the walls and base to be absorbed by the food. The cooker door and door frame are fitted with special seals to ensure that the microwaves are safely contained within the cooker. All microwaves have one or more cut-out devices so that the flow of microwave energy stops automatically whenever the door of the cooker is opened.

TYPES OF MICROWAVE COOKERS

There are three basic microwave cookers available:

Portable Microwave Cooker

This is the most popular kind, simply requiring a 13- or 15-amp plug for use. It sits neatly on a work surface, trolley or other stable surface.

Double Oven Cookers

There are a few microwave cookers available that are incorporated into conventional housings where the microwave acts as a second cooker, keeping conventional and microwave systems separate.

Combination Ovens

These ovens have the facility to cook both conventionally, and by microwave energy, in one oven. The user can operate either the microwave, the conventional oven, or both together, or even in sequence. A further choice is also available if it is fan-assisted.

MICROWAVE FEATURES

The features on microwave cookers are numerous and each is worth examining for its merits. Choose a model carefully to suit your own special needs and requirements.

Controls

The very simplest controls on a microwave cooker are likely to be a timer and a 'cook' button. To operate, simply place the food in the cooker cavity, close the door, set the timer for the cooking time required and depress the 'cook' control. The microwave cooker will continue cooking until the timer moves to the 'off' position when it will automatically stop the microwave energy. The same action would happen if you opened the cooker door during the cooking cycle. To restart, close the door and press the 'cook' button once again.

Timer Controls

Most timers span up to 30 minutes. Gradations of seconds are generally incorporated at the lower end of the scale for short cooking times where timing is critical. Often the control is a dial, sometimes it is a sliding device. Care should always be taken to set the control accurately.

Cook Control

Also called the start control, since it switches on the microwave energy.

Power Level Control

In its simplest form, this is a control that enables you to choose to cook at a slower rate than full or HIGH power. Basic microwaves with a simple on/off control always operate on 100% power input. Variable control cookers enable you to decrease this power input to varying levels (see page 17).

Indicator Lights

These are a useful visible reminder that a cooking operation has been set, is in progress or has finished.

Audible Reminders

Usually in the form of a bell or buzzer, they are a signal that the cooking time is complete.

Thermometers

Only use if the manufacturer specifically states in the handbook that it is safe to do so. Many manufacturers now supply integral thermometers or probes for microwave cooking.

Turntable

Many cookers incorporate a turntable instead of, or in addition to, the wave stirrer, to help evenly distribute microwaves through the cooker cavity. Some turntables are removable.

Door Latch

Some doors have no latch at all and have an up-and-over operation. Others have a handle, and some a push button to open the door.

SPECIAL FEATURES

Automatic Defrost

Gives food a short burst of energy followed by a rest period and then repeats the process until the food is evenly thawed. (See page 22.)

Browning Element

A browning element is sometimes incorporated in the roof of the cooker and acts just like an electric grill. Use it for pre-browning or crisping and browning foods after microwave cooking.

Keep Warm/Stay Hot Control

A control based on a very low power pulse, enables foods to be kept warm without overcooking for up to 1 hour.

Two Power-Level Cooking

This can be found in special, and more expensive, microwave cookers, where microwaves enter from the sides of the cooker rather than from the top or bottom. Two or more cooking power levels may be employed for cooking different dishes at the same time.

CARE AND CLEANING OF THE MICROWAVE COOKER

Even though there is little chance of food baking on to the cooker walls (since they stay cool) wipe up spills – if you don't, they will absorb energy.

- Wipe the cooker surfaces with a damp soapy sponge or proprietary cleaner daily to avoid stale smells.
- Regularly take out and clean removable bases, shelves and turntables.
- Do not clean surfaces with harsh abrasives – they are not necessary, and any scratches developed by using them may serve to distort the microwave pattern in the cooker.
- Replace or remove and clean any air filters or stirrer fan guards regularly.
- Do not splash water over the vents when cleaning the outer casing.

MICROWAVE EQUIPMENT

The following basic household equipment is ideal, since microwaves pass through them.

- Glass, pottery and china: for all-round general use. Check that dishes do not have a metallic trim. Pottery should be non-porous except for chicken bricks.
- Paper cookware, greaseproof paper, kitchen paper, cardboard boxes, paper napkins: use for short cooking periods, defrosting and speedy reheating. Cardboard boxes make good replacement cake 'tins'.
- Plastic cookware, ideal for short cooking times, defrosting and reheating. Do not use where high temperatures are achieved, do not use melamine plastics as they char. Use only plastics that are 'dishwasher safe'.
- Cook-in bags, cling film and 'roaster' bags: for general cooking use, defrosting and reheating; remember to replace metal ties with elastic bands or string; tie very loosely.

SPECIAL MICROWAVE EQUIPMENT

- Browning dishes are made of a glass ceramic substance with a special coating that attracts microwave energy. This dish, after preheating, browns meat and poultry and 'fries' eggs. The dish does get hot, so use oven gloves when handling.
- Defrost boxes: special see-through covered plastic boxes, complete with trivet, for efficient defrosting.
- Special microwave cookware: a range that includes almost everything that is conventionally found in metal but made in a durable plastic.
- Microwave thermometers: specially made without mercury.

TO TEST IF A DISH IS SUITABLE FOR MICROWAVE USE

If in doubt place 250 ml (8 fl oz) water in a glass jug in the dish. Cook for 1 minute on HIGH. If the water becomes hot the dish can be used. If the dish becomes hot it cannot.

ADVANTAGES OF MICROWAVE COOKING

Speed: It is possible to save up to three-quarters of normal cooking times – although generally, during most cooking operations, you'll save between one-half and two-thirds. Times and savings will depend upon size, quantity, starting temperature, shape and density of the food being cooked.

Economy: Since microwave cookers cook faster than conventional cookers, they accordingly use less power and are consequently more economical to run. There are also no lengthy and costly preheating periods required, no heavy installation costs and, with wise use, savings to be made by observing standing times for residual heat.

Efficiency: Heat is generated instantly in the food being cooked so microwave cooking is extremely efficient. There is little or no heat loss – the food receives all the energy output.

Cooler Cooking: The microwave and its utensils – with the exception of the special browning dish – stay cool during the cooking operation. The kitchen itself also stays cool – and there is less risk of accidental burns.

Smells and Cooking Odours: These are dramatically reduced because of the shorter cooking times and because they are contained within the cooker cavity. This is a great benefit when cooking strong smelling foods.

Saves Washing Up: Since it is possible to freeze, defrost, cook and serve in the same container, it follows that you have much less washing-up at the end of a meal. Food is also less likely to bake on to dishes.

Easy Cleaning: The microwave, with its easy-to-wipe surfaces, often just needs a quick wipe to keep it clean. There are fewer boil-over spillages and baked-on spatterings to deal with.

Nutritional Value and Flavour: If you follow cooking times precisely, you are unlikely to overcook foods and will keep more of their vitamin or mineral nutritional value. Colours stay bright, natural flavours are retained and fruit and vegetables remain crisp. Many foods can also be cooked without – or with the barest minimum of – additives like oil or butter, making it the perfect cooking appliance for those on special diets.

Defrosting: The microwave with its 'unfreezer' power eliminates the need to plan the defrosting of foods hours ahead. You can simply defrost and cook in one operation.

Reheating: Dried-up dishes become a thing of the past. The microwave cooker allows you to reheat ready-cooked foods in minutes. Leftovers for latecomers will taste freshly made.

Safety in Use: Microwave cookers are very simple to use and since they stay cool – and most dishes stay cool – they can be used by the young, elderly and disabled, with confidence.

Mobility: Look upon your microwave as a portable cooking aid. Providing you have a stable surface and a 13-amp or 15-amp plug you can use your microwave in the dining room, patio, garden, caravan. It can be conveniently placed on a trolley and wheeled from room to room.

MICROWAVE COOKING TECHNIQUES

To get the best results from your microwave cooker there are a few simple techniques:

Stirring Foods: in conventional cooking on the hob we stir from the bottom of the pan to the top for even cooking. In the microwave we stir from the outside of the dish, where the food generally cooks first, to the centre, which receives less energy. Stirring, however, is only occasionally required in the microwave rather than being continually essential.

Rotating Food: when a food cannot be stirred or turned over, the dish should be given a quarter-turn regularly during the cooking time, to ensure even results. This is unnecessary if your microwave has a turntable.

Arranging Foods: the success of a dish not only depends upon the ingredients used and their combination but also on the way in which they are arranged for even absorption of the energy. Arrange foods in one of the following ways for best results:

- Arrange several items of the same food, of a similar size, in a ring pattern in the cooking dish so that they receive equal energy.
- Foods that have uneven shapes like chicken pieces, chops, whole fish or fish steaks should be arranged so that the thicker portions of the food are positioned to the outer edge where they receive more energy.
- When arranging a meal on a plate for reheating at a later time then ensure that food is evenly spread out on the plate and that any dense foods or thicker portions are positioned to the outer edge.
- For even cooking and reheating try to ensure that foods are of an even depth in the dish. If not possible, rearrange once or twice.

Rearranging Foods: to ensure even cooking, you can rearrange foods in the dish halfway through the cooking – even with a turntable. Move foods from the outside of the dish to the inside.

Shielding Foods: shielding is a microwave technique used to protect vulnerable parts of a food from overcooking or from defrosting at a faster rate than the rest of the food. Foods that may need the protection of shielding include poultry wings, the heads and tails of a whole fish, the bone ends of chops, the narrow end of legs of lamb or pork and the corners of square or rectangular dishes used for baking cakes.

Use small strips of aluminium foil to protect these areas – either wrap around or secure in position with wooden cocktail sticks. This is the *only* time when small pieces of metal may be introduced into the microwave cavity, but do ensure that they do not touch the cooker lining during the cooking process.

Covering and Wrapping Foods: by covering a food during microwave cooking you can speed up the cooking process and also prevent spattering of juices on the cooker walls. There are several ways of covering foods:

- Use a tight-fitting lid to a dish or use a saucer or plate to cover.
- Use 'cook-in' bags or 'roaster' bags for vegetables and meat roasts. Remember to replace the metal ties provided with elastic bands or string.
- Cling film plastic wrap is invaluable for microwave users but do remember to puncture it before cooking to allow the escape of steam. Use it to cover all sorts of foods and, surprisingly, it will not melt.

- Absorbent kitchen paper is useful as a cover or base for moist or fatty foods. Use when cooking jacket potatoes or bacon rashers, freshening chips, warming bread or drying herbs. A damp piece of kitchen paper is also ideal for softening pancakes and steaming shellfish.

Observing Standing Times: for a time after the energy has been turned off in a microwave cooker, food will continue to cook. This is due to conduction of heat within the food – so it is important to take care not to overcook food and to allow for standing times before serving. Remember, it is very easy to cook for a little longer after standing but impossible to reverse the process! When cooking roasts, this residual heat time can be up to 20 minutes – and if a food is to be served hot, cover during standing.

Removing Excess Cooking Juices: As they attract microwave energy which would otherwise be utilized to cook the food, in effect they slow down the cooking process. It is therefore advisable to remove these juices at regular intervals. This can be done easily with a bulb baster and they can always be re-introduced if the food starts to dry out.

Releasing Pressure in Foods: it is essential to prick whole foods or foods with membranes, prior to cooking in the microwave. If certain foods are not pricked pressure mounts during the cooking process and they burst.

Foods like sausages, kidneys, jacket-baked potatoes and baked apples must therefore be pricked, while boil-in-the-bag pouches, whole fish and cling film need to be snipped or cut.

Egg yolks must also be pricked prior to cooking because they are also likely to burst.

ROASTING CHART USING MICROWAVE THERMOMETER		
Meat	Remove from cooker when this temperature reached	After standing will reach this temperature for serving
Beef: rare	55°C/130°F	65°C/150°F
medium	60°C/140°F	70°C/160°F
well-done	70°C/160°F	78°C/170°F
Pot roasts	65°C/150°F	70°C/160°F
Meat loaf	55°C/130°F	60°C/140°F
Veal	65°C/150°F	75°C/170°F
Lamb	70°C/160°F	82°C/180°F
Pork	75°C/165°F	85°C/185°F
Poultry	80°C/175°F	88°C/190°F
Ham	50°C/120°C	55°C/130°F

Cooking with a Microwave Thermometer: readily available and inexpensive, a specially designed microwave thermometer is useful for cooking foods like meat or poultry roasts, where the internal temperature indicates the degree of cooking. It looks like a traditional thermometer (but without the mercury).

Insert the microwave thermometer into the centre of the thickest muscle – ensuring it is not touching fat or bone.

A sophisticated version of the microwave thermometer is the temperature probe available on some microwaves.

Browning Foods: the browning of foods during cooking is due, in part, to a chemical reaction taking place over a period of time. In the microwave there is little surface heat, and with speedy cooking times, this browning reaction is limited.

A large turkey, cooked in the microwave, will due to its long cooking time still turn brown but small items like chops, cakes, chicken pieces and steaks do not brown so readily. In many instances, this does not matter, especially if you intend to serve meat with a gravy, sauce or coating or if you intend to ice or frost a cake. But where colour is important try one of the following tips.

- Brown under the grill before or after: roasts, gratin-style dishes, breads and biscuits.
- Cook in a special microwave browning dish: hamburgers, steaks, sausages, fish steaks, chicken pieces, fried eggs, fried sandwiches.
- Coat with a proprietary microwave browning mix: chicken pieces, roasts, sausages, burgers, grills.
- Coat with a home-made browning agent like browned breadcrumbs, paprika, colourful soup mix, brown or tomato sauce, crushed crisps or soy sauce: chicken pieces, hamburgers, roasts, grills, gratin-style dishes.
- Lay bacon rashers on roasts or burgers so that they brown during cooking.
- Include dark-coloured ingredients in the mixture: cakes, biscuits, breads, pastry items, puddings.
- Sprinkle baked items before cooking with a colourful edible mixture like cinnamon and sugar, mixed chopped glacé fruits, toasted coconut, chocolate vermicelli, chopped nuts, poppy seeds, dried herbs.
- Glaze with a fruit preserve or marmalade to add colour: hams, poultry roasts and pieces, game birds.
- Top breads, cakes and biscuits with a colourful icing or frosting after cooking and standing.

FACTORS AFFECTING COOKING TIMES

Density: The denser a food, the longer it will take to cook. A cake, for example, will cook faster than the same-sized joint of meat because it is light and porous and far less dense. This is because microwaves cannot penetrate deeply into denser foods. Denser foods do however retain heat longer – so standing times are longer.

When cooking a dish with both dense and light-structured foods, place the denser foods to the outer edge where they receive more energy.

Shape of the food: Wherever possible try to secure foods into regular shapes for cooking. Irregular shapes cook unevenly – narrower pieces cook faster than those which are thicker. Bone and roll meat of irregular shapes. Shield very vulnerable pieces with small strips of foil (see page 12).

Quantity of food: Timings given for microwave cooking relate directly to the quantity of food being cooked. For example two jacket potatoes take longer to cook than one – although not twice as long.

In general, when doubling the amount of food, increase the cooking time by one-third to one-half, and if reducing the amount of food by half, reduce time by less than one-half.

Composition of food: Fats and sugars absorb microwave energy at a greater rate than liquids and other components. Therefore foods like bacon and jam will cook faster than foods like vegetables and meats.

Right: Roast chicken with pâté stuffing (page 48)
Bottom: Baked eggs with spinach and bacon (page 32)

Foods with a low water content like breads and cakes will also cook faster.

Bones in meat: Bone is a good conductor of heat into food, therefore meat next to the bone will generally cook faster.

Height of food in the cooker: Any food positioned near to the energy source will cook faster. For even cooking, stir or rearrange during cooking.

CHECKING IF FOOD IS COOKED

Cakes and sponge puddings: often appear wet on the surface when cooked but continue cooking with the residual heat during standing time. Test by inserting a wooden cocktail stick at the *minimum* time. It is cooked if the stick comes out clean.

Jacket potatoes: these often appear firm at the end of the cooking time. Check that they give a little, when pressed with the thumb, then wrap in foil and leave to stand for 5 minutes.

Meat: this should be fork-tender and be easy to carve after standing. Use a thermometer for best results.

Chicken: juices should run clear when the thickest part of the flesh is pierced. Wrap the chicken in foil to stand.

Fish: the flesh will flake easily when cooked but at first may appear translucent, especially in the centre – this will go during the standing period.

Vegetables: these should be only fork-tender – not soft – when cooked, as they will cook during standing time.

Reheated meals: these are generally hot enough when the base of the plate feels warm to the touch.

Custards, quiches and egg-based fillings: these may appear soft or wet in the centre but will cook upon standing. Insert a knife between the centre and outer edge – if it comes out clean the dish is cooked.

Pastries: when cooked, the base of pastries should be dry and opaque.

FOODS TO AVOID COOKING IN THE MICROWAVE

Eggs in Shells: these are liable to burst.

Popcorn: this is too dry to absorb microwave energy.

Batter Recipes: items like Yorkshire puddings, soufflés, pancakes and crêpes need conventional cooking to become crisp and firm.

Meringues: these should be cooked in the conventional oven.

Deep Fat Frying: this is not recommended since it requires prolonged heating and it is difficult to control the temperatures of the fat.

Liquids in Bottles: only wide-necked bottles should be used in the microwave or they may shatter.

MICROWAVE SAFETY

* Always disconnect the cooker from the electrical supply before cleaning.
* Keep the door seals free from food, dust or grease. A good seal is important for safety.
* Buy your microwave cooker *only* from a retailer who offers a comprehensive after-sales service. For a modest outlay, you can insure against replacement parts and labour should they prove necessary after the guarantee period expires.
* Do not use or operate the cooker if it has been damaged in any way. Contact a service engineer at once.
* Do not operate the cooker when it is empty. For safety place a cup of water in the cooker when it is not in use. If the cooker is accidentally switched on the water will absorb the energy – there is then negligible risk of damaging the magnetron.

MICROWAVE TIPS

Blanching almonds: place 250 ml (8 fl oz) water in a jug. Cook on HIGH for 2½ minutes or until boiling, add the almonds and cook for ½ minute. Drain then slip skins off.

Toasting nuts: place in a browning dish and cook on HIGH for 4-5 minutes – stirring each minute.

Melting chocolate: break chocolate into pieces and place in a bowl. Cook on HIGH, for 1 minute per 25 g/1 oz.

Toasting coconut: spread 100 g/4 oz desiccated coconut on a plate. Cook on HIGH for 5-6 minutes, stirring each minute.

Peeling tomatoes: place up to six tomatoes in a ring on kitchen paper. Cook on HIGH for 10-15 seconds. STAND for 15 minutes, then peel.

Squeezing juice: to gain maximum juice from a citrus fruit, prick the skins and cook on HIGH for 5 seconds.

Flambéing with spirits: heat spirits in a jug on HIGH for 15 seconds. It will then ignite more easily.

Softening jams and spreads: cook on HIGH for about 5-10 seconds per 500 g/1 lb.

Dissolving gelatine: soak gelatine in water until spongy. Cook on HIGH for about ½ minute or until clear.

Peeling peaches and apricots: place up to 4 peaches in a bowl with very little water. Cover and cook on HIGH for 1-1½ minutes. Leave to STAND for 5 minutes, drain and peel.

Warming a baby's bottle: invert the teat and cook on HIGH for 1 minute.

Drying herbs and citrus rinds: place on a plate and cook on HIGH until dry.

Clarifying Crystallized Honey: cook on HIGH for 1-2 minutes. Stir well.

Softening butter: cook on HIGH for 5 seconds then STAND for 5 minutes.

CONVERTING CONVENTIONAL RECIPES

A great many of your favourite family recipes can be converted for use in the microwave simply by adjusting, and often shortening, the recipe cooking time. The ideal way to start to convert a recipe is to study the recipe carefully and check whether there are any familiar techniques in its method such as roasting, steaming or poaching that you can easily convert. Check that all the ingredients included can be cooked in the microwave and refer to procedures and times from other standard recipes to work out your cooking times.

The following checklist will help you with conversion, but use it only as a guideline – rely upon your own judgment for best results.

- In general terms, foods cooked in the microwave take about one-quarter to one-third of the time they take when cooking conventionally. But do, however, allow for standing times.
- Check the cooking process regularly. Stir and rearrange foods if they appear to be cooking unevenly.
- Use less liquids when cooking items like stews, casseroles and soups and in cooking vegetables.
- Foods tend to rise higher during microwave cooking so, in general, choose larger containers.
- Reduce flavourings like herbs and spices by about one-third since the flavours of these seem to be brought out more strongly by microwave cooking.
- Wherever possible cut food into small, even-sized pieces so that they are small and uniform for quick cooking.

MENU PLANNING

As a general rule, aim to cook the main course first. Most meat, fish and poultry dishes, especially those cooked in sauces, do improve upon standing and can be quickly reheated.

Obviously, foods that require a long standing time or lengthy cooking time should be cooked first. Last-minute or quick-cooking dishes can be cooked in that standing time. For ease of preparation and cooking, prepare starters and desserts well ahead and reheat if necessary, just before serving. A pudding can also be cooked while you are eating the starter or main course if it requires little attention.

RECIPE GUIDELINES

The recipes that follow have been created and tested using a 600 Watt microwave cooker with turntable, on three power settings – DEFROST, MEDIUM and HIGH. (If yours does not have a turntable then remember to turn dishes occasionally for even results.)

HIGH power is used for most general high-speed cooking operations.

MEDIUM power is used for slower cooking of sensitive foods. It is also employed for cooking foods that require tenderizing over a longer period such as meat in casseroles.

DEFROST power is used, as the name suggests, to defrost foods but can also be used to cook delicate dishes.

If your microwave cooker differs from these settings refer to the chart below which is a handy guide to comparative control settings. Consult your microwave handbook to find out the power levels that apply to your microwave. As a general rule: if you have a 500 Watt microwave cooker, add about 20 seconds to each whole minute of cooking time, and if you have a 700 Watt microwave cooker, decrease the cooking time by about 15 seconds per minute.

GUIDE TO COMPARATIVE CONTROL SETTINGS							
Description used in this book		DEFROST			MEDIUM		HIGH
Descriptions on popular microwave cookers	1 Keep warm	2 Simmer	3 Stew	4 Defrost	5 Bake	6 Roast	7 Full/high
Approx. power output in Watts	150w	200w	250w	300w	450w	500-550w	600-700w
Comparative cooking time in minutes	4	3¼	2½	2	1¾	1¾	1
	8	6¾	5	4	3¼	2¾	2
	12	10	7½	6	5	4	3
	16	13¼	10	8	6¾	5¼	4
	20	16¾	12½	10	8¼	6¾	5
	24	20	15	12	10	8	6
	28	23¼	17½	14	11¾	9¼	7
	32	26¾	20	16	13¼	10¾	8
	36	30	22½	18	15	12	9
	40	33¼	25	20	16½	13¼	10
(For times greater than these, add the figures in the appropriate columns together)							

MICROWAVE COOKING GUIDE	COOKING TIME IN MINUTES ON HIGH (per 500 g/1 lb)	COOKING NOTES
FISH		
Cod and haddock fillets	6-8	Place the fillet tails to the centre of the dish or shield with foil. Cut the skin in two or three places.
steaks	5-6	Cover with greaseproof paper.
Salmon steaks	5-6	Cover with greaseproof paper.
Whole salmon	8-9	Shield the head and tail with foil. Cut the skin in two or three places.
Scallops	6-8	Cover with damp kitchen paper.
Smoked haddock	5-6	Cover with cling film, snipping two holes to allow the steam to escape.
Whole trout	6-8	Shield the head and tail with foil, cut the skin in two or three places. Or, see page 66.
REHEATING BOILED SHELLFISH		
Lobster tails	6-7	Turn tails over halfway through the cooking time.
Whole lobster	7-9	Allow to stand for 5 minutes before serving. Turn over halfway through.
Prawns, shrimps and scampi	3-5	Arrange the peeled shellfish in a ring in a shallow dish and cover with cling film, snipping two holes in the top to allow the steam to escape.
POULTRY AND GAME		
Whole chicken	6-7	Shield the tips of the wings and legs with foil. Place in a roasting bag in a dish with 2-3 tablespoons stock.
Chicken pieces (each): 1 2 4 6	3-5 5-7 7-11 9-15	Place the meatiest part of the chicken piece to the outside of the dish. Cover with greaseproof paper.
Duck	6-7	Shield the tips of the wings, tail end and legs with foil. Prick the skin thoroughly to help release the fat. Place in a dish on a trivet in a roasting bag and turn over halfway through.
Grouse, guinea fowl, partridge, pheasant, pigeon, poussin, quail and woodcock	8-9	Shield the tips of the wings and legs with foil. Smear the breast with butter and place in a roasting bag in a dish.
Turkey	7-8	Shield the tips of the wings and legs with foil. Place in a roasting bag in a dish with 2-3 tablespoons stock. Turn over at least once during cooking. Or, see page 70.

MICROWAVE COOKING GUIDE	COOKING TIME IN MINUTES ON HIGH (per 500 g/1 lb)		COOKING NOTES
BEEF			
Topside	Rare:	5	Choose a good quality joint with an even covering of fat, and a neat shape. Allow to stand for 15-20 minutes, wrapped in foil, before carving.
	Medium:	6-7	
	Well-done:	8-10	
Rib	Rare:	6½	Ideally, bone and roll the joint before cooking. Stand for 15-20 minutes, wrapped in foil, before carving.
	Medium:	8-9	
	Well-done:	10-11	
Minced beef	5		
Rump and fillet steak	Rare:	2	Preheat a browning dish according to the manufacturer's instructions. Add the meat and brown. Turn over and cook for the recommended time.
	Medium:	2-4	
	Well-done:	4	
Beefburgers (each):			Preheat a browning dish according to the manufacturer's instructions. Add the beefburgers and cook for the recommended time, turning them over halfway through recommended cooking time.
100 g/4 oz × 1	3		
100 g/4 oz × 2	4-5		
LAMB			
Leg	7-9		As beef joints.
Loin or chump chops (each):			Preheat the browning dish according to the manufacturer's instructions. Add the chops and cook, turning over halfway through the cooking time.
2	7-8		
4	8-10		
6	16-18		
PORK			
Leg	10-12		Cover pointed end with foil. Score fat with a sharp knife and sprinkle with salt to get a crisp crackling. Allow to stand for 20 minutes, wrapped in foil. Brown under a grill to crisp if liked.
Loin	11-14		Roll into a neat shape before cooking. Stand for 20 minutes, covered.
Loin or chump chops			As lamb chops.
BACON OR GAMMON			
Joint	7-8		Cook in a browning dish or cover with cling film. Turn halfway through.
Gammon steaks (each)	3-4		
Bacon 4 slices	3-4		Place on a plate or bacon rack and cover with absorbent kitchen paper. Turn rashers over halfway through cooking time.
Offal	5-6		Prick well before cooking.
Sausages			Prick thoroughly and arrange on a rack or plate. Cover with absorbent kitchen paper and turn halfway through cooking time.
2	2-3		
4	4		

MICROWAVE GUIDE TO COOKING FROZEN AND FRESH VEGETABLES

TYPE OF VEGETABLES AND QUANTITY	WATER/SALT	COOKING TIME (in minutes on HIGH)		COOKING NOTES
		FROZEN	FRESH	
Asparagus				Place in a dish arranging any thicker stems to the outside of the dish. Cover to cook.
225 g/8 oz	1½ tbs/¼ tsp	7-8	9-10	
500 g/1 lb	3 tbs/½ tsp	8-10	13-15	
Aubergines				Cover to cook. Stir the cubed aubergine after 3 minutes.
2 medium, halved	1 tbs/¼ tsp	9-11	8-10	
1 whole, peeled and cubed	1 tbs/¼ tsp	11-12	6-7	
Beans				Cover to cook. Stir the beans twice during the cooking. Test after the minimum time.
225 g/8 oz	2 tbs/¼ tsp	7-8	10-12	
500 g/1 lb	4 tbs/½ tsp	9-10	15-17	
Beetroot				Cover to cook. Stir or rearrange halfway. Stand for 10 minutes before peeling.
2 medium	4 tbs/½ tsp	N/A	13-16	
5 medium	4 tbs/½ tsp		23-26	
Broccoli				Place in a dish arranging the stalks to the outside. Cover to cook. Stir after 6 minutes.
225 g/8 oz	2 tbs/—	7-8	8-10	
500 g/1 lb	4 tbs/—	9-10	11-13	
Brussels sprouts				Trim away any damaged or coarse leaves and cut large sprouts in half. Cover to cook. Stir after 4 minutes cooking time.
225 g/8 oz	1 tbs/¼ tsp	7-8	8-10	
500 g/1 lb	2 tbs/½ tsp	9-10	11-13	
Cabbage, shredded				Use a large dish and ensure that the cabbage fits loosely. Cover to cook. Stir or rearrange halfway through.
225 g/8 oz	2 tbs/¼ tsp	4-5	9-10	
500 g/1 lb	4 tbs/½ tsp	6-7	11-13	
Carrots, whole				Stir or rearrange halfway through the cooking time. Cut carrots into 1 cm/½ in thick slices. Slicing diagonally reduces the cooking time by 2 minutes. Cover to cook.
225 g/8 oz	2 tbs/¼ tsp	6-7	13-15	
500 g/1 lb	4 tbs/½ tsp	8-10	19-21	
sliced				
225 g/8 oz	2 tbs/¼ tsp	5-6	10-12	
500 g/1 lb	4 tbs/½ tsp	6-8	13-15	
Cauliflower, whole				Cover to cook. Turn a whole cauliflower or stir florets halfway through the cooking time. Allow whole cauliflower to stand for 5 minutes.
1 medium about 675 g/1½ lb	4 tbs/½ tsp	N/A	13-17	
florets				
225 g/8 oz	2 tbs/¼ tsp	7-8	8-10	
500 g/1 lb	4 tbs/½ tsp	9-10	11-13	
Celery, whole or sliced				Cover to cook. Stir halfway through the cooking time.
500 g/1 lb	2 tbs/¼ tsp	N/A	15-17	
Courgettes, sliced whole				Cover to cook. Dot lightly with 25 g/1 oz butter before cooking. Stir or rearrange halfway through the cooking time.
500 g/1 lb	—	5-6	6-7	
6 small whole	—	—	8	
Leeks, sliced				Cover to cook. Stir halfway through the cooking time.
500 g/1 lb	2 tbs/½ tsp	9-10	11-13	

MICROWAVE GUIDE TO COOKING FROZEN AND FRESH VEGETABLES

TYPE OF VEGETABLES AND QUANTITY	WATER/SALT	COOKING TIME (in minutes on HIGH)		COOKING NOTES
		FROZEN	FRESH	
Mushrooms, whole or sliced 225 g/8 oz 500 g/1 lb	1 tbs water or butter	4-5 8	3-5 5-7	Cover to cook. Add salt, if liked, after cooking. Stir halfway through the cooking time.
Parsnips 500 g/1 lb	4 tbs/½ tsp	8-9	9-11	Cover to cook. Stir halfway through the cooking time.
Peas, shelled 225 g/8 oz 500 g/1 lb	2 tbls/¼ tsp 4 tbs/½ tsp	5-6 8-9	8-10 10-12	Cover to cook. Stir halfway through. Add 15-25 g/½-1 oz butter after cooking and stand for 5 minutes before serving.
Potatoes, peeled and quartered 500 g/1 lb	4 tbs/½ tsp	N/A	11-15	Cover to cook. Stir twice during cooking.
Spinach 500 g/1 lb	—	8-9	7-9	Wash but do not dry before cooking in a roasting bag.
Sweetcorn 500 g/1 lb	4 tbs/½ tsp	8-9	N/A	Cover to cook.
Tomatoes (halved)	Salt to taste	N/A	1½-2	Cover to cook.
Turnips, cubed 500 g/1 lb	4 tbs/¼ tsp	12-13	13-15	Stir twice during cooking.

MICROWAVE GUIDE TO COOKING FRUIT

TYPE OF FRUIT	COOKING TIME IN MINUTES ON HIGH (per 500 g/1 lb)		PREPARATION (Stir fruit once or twice during cooking and leave to stand for 5 minutes)
	FROZEN	FRESH	
Apricots	4-8	8	Stone and wash, then sprinkle with 100 g/4 oz sugar.
Berry fruits	4-6	4-5	Top and tail or hull. Wash and add 100 g/4 oz sugar.
Cooking apples	4-8	8	Peel, core and slice, then sprinkle with 100 g/4 oz sugar.
Peaches	4-8	6	As apricots.
Pears 6 medium-sized	8-12	10-11	Peel, halve and core. Dissolve 75 g/3 oz sugar in a little water and pour over the pears.
Plums, cherries or damsons	8-12	5-6	As apricots.
Rhubarb	7-8	9-11	Cut into short lengths. Add 100 g/4 oz sugar and the grated rind 1 lemon.

DEFROSTING

It is not surprising that the microwave has also been called the 'freezer companion' since it quickly and efficently defrosts frozen foods in minutes rather than hours – effectively opening the door to many last-minute meals.

Most manufacturers of microwave cookers have incorporated a special DEFROST power control or button. This is designed to introduce just the right amount of microwave energy into a food, over a given period of time, so that it is automatically defrosted without fear of too much moisture loss, over-cooking or bacterial growth.

If your cooker does not have this facility then it is still possible to simulate its action by turning it on and off, at regular intervals, with rest periods in between, until the food is evenly defrosted.

The recipes and charts in this section refer to a microwave cooker with DEFROST control and timings are accurate. However, the following tips will ensure first-rate even results every time.

- Defrost food slowly (do not be tempted to use a higher power control) so that it does not begin to cook on the outside before it is completely thawed.
- Transfer any foods which have been frozen in foil trays or containers into a suitable microwave dish before defrosting. Also remember to remove any metal ties.
- Pierce any cling film, boil-in-bag pouches, skins or membranes prior to defrosting.
- Turn foods over during defrosting – about halfway through the time. If it is not possible to turn items over, then rearrange items wherever possible.
- Separate any blocks of frozen foods like sausage links, burgers and fish cakes as they defrost.
- Remove any defrosting juices or drips from foods as they thaw – this is best done with a bulb baster. If they are left they will only continue to attract microwave energy – increasing the defrosting time quite considerably.
- Remove giblets from poultry and game birds as they defrost.
- Open all cartons and remove any lids from items prior to defrosting.
- Items like bread, cakes and pastry benefit from being placed on a double sheet of absorbent kitchen paper during defrosting to absorb excess moisture. Alternatively, place on a microwave roasting rack or trivet.
- Blocks of food like minced beef or shellfish should be broken up with a fork during defrosting so that the frozen core will defrost quickly and evenly.
- Items like large meat joints, whole fish and whole birds should be defrosted until just icy then left to defrost completely at normal room temperature.

- Always observe a standing time period – foods will continue to cook or defrost due to heat conduction even when the microwave cooker has been turned off. So, defrost until *just* icy and allow to stand in order to produce an evenly defrosted food.
- Thin and vulnerable parts of a food like poultry wings, fish tails and the narrow end of a leg of pork or lamb, may defrost more quickly than thicker parts and even begin to cook. Shield these areas with small strips of foil during defrosting. (See page 12.) Wrap the foil around the area after it has defrosted or attach with a wooden cocktail stick.
- If defrosting and cooking in one operation then remember to stir the defrosted food from the outside to the centre of the dish, or rearrange the food once or twice during the defrosting and cooking time.

DEFROSTING GUIDE	POWER SETTING	TIME (in mins)	INSTRUCTIONS
MEAT			
Beef			
Joints 500 g/1 lb	DEFROST	9	Turn over at least once.
Fillet 500 g/1 lb	DEFROST	8	
Sirloin 500 g/1 lb	DEFROST	8	
Minced beef 500 g/1 lb	DEFROST	5-7	Break up with a fork during defrosting.
Lamb			
Joints 500 g/1 lb	DEFROST	10	Turn over at least once.
Chops 500 g/1 lb	DEFROST	5	
Pork			
Joints 500 g/1 lb	DEFROST	10	Turn over at least once.
Chops 500 g/1 lb	DEFROST	5	
Veal			
Joints 500 g/1 lb	DEFROST	9	Turn over at least once.
Offal 500 g/1 lb	DEFROST	2-3	Turn over and rearrange at least once.
Bacon			
1 (225 g/8 oz) pkt	DEFROST	2-3	Turn over halfway through.
1 (500 g/1 lb) joint	DEFROST	8	
Casserole and vegetables			
4 portions	HIGH	15-17	To thaw *and reheat*.
Sausages			
Thick 500 g/1 lb	DEFROST	5-6	Turn over and rearrange halfway through defrosting. Stand 5 minutes.
Shepherd's pie			
400 g/14 oz	HIGH	6	To thaw *and reheat*. Allow to stand 2 minutes then cook a further 6-7 minutes.
Roast meat and gravy			
350 g/12 oz	HIGH	4	To thaw *and reheat*. Allow to stand 3 minutes then cook a further 4 minutes.
POULTRY AND GAME			
Chicken			
Whole 500 g/1 lb	DEFROST	6	Shield the wing tips with foil. Place the meatiest part of the chicken pieces to the outside. Turn over halfway through the defrosting time.
Pieces 500 g/1 lb	DEFROST	5	
Duck 500 g/1 lb	DEFROST	4-6	Shield the wings, tail and legs with foil.
Small game birds	DEFROST	5-6	Shield the tips of the wings and legs with foil. Turn over halfway through.
Turkey 500 g/1 lb	DEFROST	6-7	Shield the tips of the wings and leg with foil. Turn over twice during the defrosting time. Shield any warm spots with foil during defrosting.

DEFROSTING GUIDE	POWER SETTING	TIME (in mins)	INSTRUCTIONS
FISH			
Fillets 500 g/1 lb	DEFROST	4-5	Turn over and rearrange halfway through.
Steaks			
1 (175 g/6 oz)	DEFROST	2	Turn over and rearrange
2 (175 g/6 oz)	DEFROST	3-4	halfway through.
Whole fish			
1 (225-275 g/8-10 oz)	DEFROST	6-8	Turn over halfway through.
1 (1.5-1.75 kg/3-4 lb)	DEFROST	16-20	
SHELLFISH			
Crabmeat 500 g/1 lb	DEFROST	5-7	Break up with fork during defrosting.
Lobster whole			
500 g/1 lb	DEFROST	12	Trim over halfway through.
Prawns, Shrimp and Scampi			
500 g/1 lb	DEFROST	5-7	Rearrange halfway through defrosting time.
Scallops 500 g/1 lb	DEFROST	5-7	Rearrange halfway through defrosting time.
SOUPS			
600 ml (1 pint)	HIGH	6-8	To thaw *and* reheat. Break block during thawing and reheating time.
BREAD			
1 large unsliced loaf	DEFROST	6-8	Allow to stand 5-10 minutes. Turn over once.
1 large sliced loaf	DEFROST	10-12	Allow to stand 10-15 minutes. Turn several times.
CAKES AND BISCUITS			
225 g/8 oz	DEFROST	1-3	Allow to stand for at least 5 minutes.
SAUCES			
300 ml (½ pint)	HIGH	6-8	To thaw *and reheat*. Stir twice. Whisk.
STOCK			
300 ml (½ pint)	HIGH	3-4	Break down frozen block during defrosting.
MISCELLANEOUS			
Butter			
250 g/9 oz block	DEFROST	1-2	Turn over once and allow to stand for at least 5 minutes.
Pâté			
1 (198 g/7 oz) pack	DEFROST	4	Allow to stand for at least 15 minutes.
Pizza			
Family size	HIGH	3-5	To thaw *and* reheat. Stand on paper towel.
Yoghurt			
1 small carton	DEFROST	3-4	Remove lid. Stir for 1 minute after defrosting to mix.

SOUPS AND STARTERS

Here is a collection of recipes to show how versatile your microwave cooker can be. There are soups for lunch, supper, or dinner party menus that are quick to make and quicker to reheat, tasting freshly made each time. As they are cooked in the serving dishes, there are no dirty saucepans to cope with. And food does not stick to the dishes and burn. Remember that liquids cooked this way retain their heat longer, so allow to cool a little before tasting or serving.

The microwave is invaluable in the making of starters, as many quick but impressive dishes can be made at the last minute while the main course, a roast for example, is standing. Even traditional pâtés and terrines can be made more rapidly – using the model given here many other classic recipes can be adapted for the microwave cooker (see page 16) with facility.

Meaty minestrone

Serves 4-6

75 g/3 oz frozen sliced onion, or 1 onion, sliced
225 g/8 oz frozen diced mixed root vegetables, or the equivalent in freshly prepared root vegetables
100 g/4 oz frozen green beans, or fresh beans
75 g/3 oz frozen sliced carrots, or 2 carrots peeled and sliced
2 sticks celery, sliced and blanched
175 g/6 oz frozen free-flow minced beef
2 tablespoons oil
2 beef stock cubes, crumbled
600 ml/1 pint boiling water
2 tablespoons chopped fresh parsley
pepper
15 g/½ oz small dried pasta shapes
To garnish
3 tablespoons freshly grated Parmesan cheese

1 Place the vegetables, beef and oil in a large bowl. Cover and cook on HIGH for 4 minutes.

2 Dissolve the stock cubes in the boiling water, stir in the parsley and season to taste.

3 Pour this stock over the mixed vegetables and stir in the pasta shapes. Cover, puncture the top and cook on HIGH for 7 minutes.

4 Sprinkle with Parmesan cheese.

Note: This soup makes a substantial lunchtime snack or family supper starter when served with Hot herb bread, Croûtons (page 33) or hot French bread.

Variations

Add a few drops of Worcestershire sauce for a winter-warming flavour. Use minced lamb instead of beef, add 100 g/4 oz frozen peas to the boiling water with the stock cubes and omit the cheese. Add mint with the parsley. Substitute a mixture of 100 g/4 oz minced pork and 50 g/2 oz diced cooked ham instead of the beef. Serve with slices of crisped bread with mustard butter.

▌ Summer leaf soup

Meaty minestrone (left), Summer leaf soup and Croûtons (page 33).

Serves 4

2 tablespoons oil
6 spring onions, chopped
1 bunch watercress, roughly chopped
225 g/8 oz frozen spinach, defrosted
100 g/4 oz frozen peas
600 ml/1 pint vegetable stock
1 tablespoon chopped fresh mint
150 ml/¼ pint grapefruit juice
salt and pepper

To garnish

½ cucumber, peeled and diced
fresh mint sprigs

1 Place the oil in a large bowl with the vegetables. Cover with cling film and cook on HIGH for 6 minutes.
2 Add the stock, cover again, puncturing the top and cook on HIGH for 3 minutes.
3 Pour the mixture into a blender or food processor and blend until smooth. Pour into a clean bowl and stir in the mint and grapefruit juice.
4 Cook on HIGH for 4 minutes. Season and serve hot or chilled, garnished with cucumber and mint.

27

▌ Carrot and orange soup

Serves 6
350 g/12 oz frozen sliced carrots, or
* 4 carrots peeled and sliced*
120 ml/4 fl oz water
100 g/4 oz frozen sliced onion, or
* 1 large onion, chopped*
1 stick celery, chopped
1 teaspoon sugar
2 tablespoons oil
175 ml/6 fl oz unsweetened orange juice
2 chicken stock cubes
900 ml/1 ½ pints boiling water
2 whole cloves
1 teaspoon ground coriander
1 teaspoon lemon juice
284 ml/10 fl oz carton double cream
salt and pepper
To garnish
thin shreds of orange rind, blanched

1 Place the carrots in a large bowl with the water, onion, celery, sugar and oil. Cover with cling film and place in the microwave cooker.
2 Cook on HIGH for 10 minutes, turning and stirring if necessary, then STAND for 2 minutes.
3 Transfer the ingredients to a blender or food processor, add the orange juice, stock cubes and half the water. Blend until smooth.
4 Pour into a large clean bowl, stir in the remaining boiling water, the cloves, coriander, lemon juice and cream. Season lightly with salt and pepper.
5 Cover the bowl again, puncture the top and cook on MEDIUM for 4 minutes. Stir and leave to STAND for 2 minutes.
6 Remove cloves, adjust the seasoning, stir again and serve garnished with orange rind.

▌ Curried apple soup

Serves 4-6
1 large onion, chopped
500 g/1 lb frozen apple slices
2 teaspoons curry powder,
* or to taste*
2 tablespoons oil
900 ml/1 ½ pints boiling water
2 chicken stock cubes
2 egg yolks
142 ml/5 fl oz carton double cream
salt and pepper
1-2 teaspoons lemon juice
a few drops of green food colouring
* (optional)*
To garnish
watercress sprigs or toasted flaked
* almonds*

1 Place onion, apple, curry powder and oil in a large bowl. Cover with cling film, puncture the top and cook on HIGH for 4 minutes.
2 Pour half the boiling water into a blender or food processor, add the stock cubes and apple mixture and blend until smooth. Pour into a large clean bowl and stir in the rest of the boiling water and mix well to combine.
3 In a separate bowl, whisk together the egg yolks and cream and season lightly with salt and pepper. Sharpen with a little lemon juice and add a drop or two of green food colouring, if liked.
4 Stir the egg yolk mixture into the rest of the soup, cover again and cook on MEDIUM for 3 minutes. (The soup must not be allowed to boil after adding egg yolks and cream.)
5 Stir and serve, garnished with watercress sprigs or some toasted flaked almonds.

Corn chowder

Serves 4
40 g/1 ½ oz butter
100 g/4 oz frozen sliced onion, or 1 large
  onion, chopped
225 g/8 oz potato, peeled and diced
3 tablespoons plain flour
2 tablespoons chopped fresh parsley
1 teaspoon turmeric
¼ teaspoon ground nutmeg or
  mace
2 fish stock cubes
750 ml/1 ¼ pints boiling water
225 g/8 oz frozen smoked haddock,
  skinned and cubed
225 g/8 oz frozen sweetcorn
salt and pepper

1 Place butter in a large bowl and
  cook on HIGH for 45 seconds until
  melted.
2 Add onion and potato, turning to
  coat them with butter. Cover bowl
  with cling film and cook on HIGH
  for 2 minutes.
3 Stir in the flour, parsley, turmeric
  and nutmeg or mace and allow the
  mixture to STAND while dissolving
  the fish stock cubes in the boiling
  water.
4 Gradually stir fish stock into the rest
  of the ingredients, add the fish and
  corn and stir well.
5 Cover again, puncture the top and
  cook on HIGH for 6 minutes,
  stirring halfway through.
6 Season to taste with salt and
  pepper and serve with hot crusty
  bread.

Variations
If fish stock cubes are difficult to
obtain, use vegetable or chicken stock
cubes instead. Try cooked rice instead
of potatoes.

Matelote provençale

Serves 4-6
225 g/8 oz frozen haddock fillet
225 g/8 oz frozen cod or whiting fillet
3 tablespoons olive oil
1 stick celery, sliced
100 g/4 oz frozen sliced onion, or 1 large
  onion, sliced
1 clove garlic, peeled and crushed
2 tablespoons plain flour
397 g/14 oz can tomatoes
2 teaspoons lemon juice
1 tablespoon chopped fresh parsley
2 bay leaves
2 fish stock cubes
300 ml/½ pint boiling water
100 g/4 oz cooked shelled mussels
75 g/3 oz frozen peeled prawns, defrosted
142 ml/5 fl oz carton double cream
150 ml/¼ pint dry white wine
150 ml/¼ pint milk
salt and pepper

1 Skin the fillets while frozen. Set aside.
2 Place oil, celery, onion and garlic in
  a shallow dish and mix well. Cover
  and cook on HIGH for 2 minutes.
3 Stir in the flour, the tomatoes with
  their juice, and transfer to a large
  clean bowl. Add lemon juice,
  parsley and bay leaves and mix well.
4 In a jug, dissolve the stock cubes in
  the water, then gradually stir into
  mixture. Cover, puncture and cook
  on HIGH for 3 minutes. Stir well.
5 Cut the fish into chunks and add
  with the mussels, prawns, cream,
  wine and milk. Stir to mix and cook
  on MEDIUM for 6 minutes. Do not
  allow to boil.
6 Stir gently, return to the microwave
  and cook on MEDIUM for 3 minutes.
  Season and STAND for 2 minutes.
  Remove bay leaves and serve hot
  with French bread.

Cheddar herb dumplings.

Cheddar herb dumplings

Serves 4
100 g/4 oz self-raising flour
50 g/2 oz shredded suet
2 tablespoons chopped fresh mixed herbs
* or 2 teaspoons dried mixed herbs*
½ teaspoon salt
¼ teaspoon pepper
65 ml/2½ fl oz cold water
12 small cubes of mature Cheddar cheese
600 ml/1 pint boiling water (for cooking)
50 g/2 oz finely ground mixed nuts
2 tablespoons chopped parsley
To serve
radicchio or lettuce leaves
redcurrant or cranberry jelly

1 Place the flour, suet and herbs in a large bowl. Season with salt and pepper, add enough water to mix to a soft but not sticky dough.
2 Divide the dough into twelve pieces and wrap each one round a cube of cheese. Form each piece into a ball.

3 Pour 600 ml/1 pint boiling water into a large bowl. Float the dumplings on the top and cook on HIGH for 4 minutes. Remove and drain on kitchen paper.
4 Roll each dumpling in the ground nuts or parsley and serve, allowing 3 per person, on radicchio (red endive) or lettuce leaves and with redcurrant or cranberry jelly.

Prawn and cashew stir-fry

Serves 4
50 g/2 oz butter
3 spring onions, trimmed and sliced
½ red pepper, finely diced
2 tablespoons chopped fresh mixed herbs
* (chives, parsley, dill)*
175 g/6 oz frozen peeled prawns,
* defrosted*
50 g/2 oz cashew nuts
For the sauce
2 tablespoons sesame oil
2 tablespoons soy sauce
2 teaspoons soft brown sugar
2 teaspoons lemon juice
½ teaspoon ground ginger
salt and pepper
To garnish
a sprinkling of chopped fresh herbs

1 Place butter in a bowl and cook on HIGH for 1 minute until melted.
2 Stir in spring onions, diced pepper and the herbs. Cook on HIGH for 2 minutes. Add the prawns and cashew nuts and set aside.
3 For the sauce: mix together the oil, soy sauce, sugar, lemon juice and ginger. Season with salt and pepper, then stir the sauce into the bowl with the prawns and nuts. Make sure the prawns are well covered by the sauce.

4 Cook on HIGH for 2-3 minutes. Serve in small individual dishes garnished with fresh herbs.

Variation

For a more substantial dish, add 2 carrots, peeled and thinly sliced, then blanched for 2 minutes on HIGH. Then add 175 g/6 oz bean sprouts, and 6-8 canned water chestnuts, thinly sliced, at stage 3.

Mock game terrine

Serves 10-12

225 g/8 oz streaky bacon rashers, rind
* removed, stretched with a knife*
1 onion, finely chopped
2 garlic cloves, crushed with a little salt
500 g/1 lb frozen diced pork
100 g/4 oz frozen lamb's liver, defrosted
* and finely chopped*
2 eggs
2 tablespoons cranberry sauce
1-2 tablespoons brandy or sherry
1-2 tablespoons dried mixed herbs
1 teaspoon mixed spice
salt and pepper

Prawn and cashew stir-fry (left) and Mock game terrine.

1 Line the base and sides of a 1 litre/ 1¾ pint loaf dish with bacon strips, leaving a good 5-6 cm/2 inch overlap around the sides and reserving 2 bacon strips for the top.
2 Mince together the onion, garlic, pork and liver, or work in a food processor until finely minced (if using a blender, add 1 egg at this stage).
3 Beat in the eggs, cranberry sauce, brandy or sherry, herbs and spice. Season lightly with salt and pepper.
4 Put 1 teaspoon of the mixture in a small dish or ramekin and cook on MEDIUM for 2 minutes. Taste and adjust the seasoning.
5 Pour the mixture into the lined dish and fold the ends of the bacon strips over the top. Lay the reserved bacon strips on top to neaten.
6 Cover the dish with cling film, puncture the top and cook on MEDIUM for 15 minutes.
7 Place a weight on top and leave the terrine to cool.

Baked eggs with spinach and bacon

Serves 4
225 g/8 oz frozen leaf spinach, defrosted
4 rashers streaky bacon, rinds removed
  and chopped
1 tablespoon olive oil
salt and pepper
4 large eggs
4 tablespoons double cream
To garnish
a sprinkling of paprika or nutmeg
8 thin toast triangles

1 Put the spinach into a sieve and press well with the back of a wooden spoon to squeeze out any excess moisture.
2 Place it in a bowl with the bacon, olive oil and salt and pepper to taste then mix well. Divide the mixture between 4 small round or oval dishes, making a hollow in the centre of each.
3 Crack an egg into each hollow and carefully prick the yolks. Spoon a tablespoon of the cream over each.
4 Cook on HIGH for 3 minutes, rearranging dishes halfway through.
5 Serve garnished with paprika or nutmeg and hand toast separately.

Suffolk smokies

Serves 4-6
225 g/8 oz frozen smoked haddock,
  skinned and defrosted
300 ml/½ pint Basic white sauce (page 58)
3 tablespoons natural yoghurt
50 g/2 oz mature Cheddar cheese, grated
a little made English mustard
salt and pepper
To garnish
parsley sprigs or a sprinkling of cayenne

1 Cut the fish into cubes. Combine the white sauce and the yoghurt, then stir the fish into the sauce. Add half the cheese and a little made English mustard to taste. Season lightly with pepper and salt, if necessary.
2 Divide the mixture between 4 individual ramekin dishes and sprinkle with the rest of the cheese. Cook, uncovered, on HIGH for 3 minutes. Check fish is cooked and, if necessary, cook on HIGH for a further 2 minutes.
3 Serve garnished with parsley or cayenne, and with triangles of brown toast.

Variations
Use unsmoked white fish. Flavour the sauce with curry powder to taste and a pinch of turmeric. Mix a little cayenne into the cheese before sprinkling over the top.

Stuffed mushrooms

Serves 4
8 large open, flat mushrooms, wiped
25 g/1 oz butter
For the stuffing
2 tablespoons finely chopped spring onion
50 g/2 oz cooked ham, finely chopped
1 heaped teaspoon finely chopped fresh
  mixed herbs or 1 teaspoon dried mixed
  herbs
½ teaspoon finely chopped garlic clove
75 g/3 oz mature Cheddar cheese, grated
salt and pepper

1 First make the stuffing: place the onion in a bowl with the ham, herbs, garlic and 50 g/2 oz of the cheese. Add salt and pepper to taste and mix well.

2 Remove stalks from mushrooms and chop them finely, then mix them into the stuffing.

3 Spoon the stuffing mixture into the hollows in the mushrooms, pressing it down gently with the back of a spoon. Set the mushrooms aside in a wide shallow dish.

4 Put the butter into a small bowl and cook on HIGH for 30 seconds until melted. Brush the butter over the stuffed mushrooms.

5 Cover the dish with cling film and cook on HIGH for 4 minutes. Serve sprinkled with the remaining grated cheese.

Croûtons

Serves 4
25 g/1 oz butter
1 slice of bread from a thickly sliced large white or brown loaf, or 2 slices from a smaller loaf

1 Place the butter in a bowl and cook on HIGH for 40 seconds, until melted.

2 Trim the crusts from the bread and cut the slices into neat 1 cm/½ inch dice. Toss in the melted butter and cook on HIGH for 1 minute. Stir and cook on HIGH for a further 1 minute. STAND for 2 minutes to crisp before serving.

Note: to dry the bread and make it easier to cut into cubes, cook on HIGH for 15-30 seconds, depending on freshness.

Slimmers' croûtons
Cook the bread cubes, without butter, on HIGH for 1 minute. Stir and cook for a further 1 minute until dry. STAND for one minute.

Hot herb loaf

Serves 4-6
25 cm/10 inch piece cut from a frozen French loaf, defrosted
50 g/2 oz butter
2 teaspoons dried mixed herbs or 1 tablespoon mixed chopped fresh herbs

1 Place the butter in a bowl and add the herbs. Cook on DEFROST until the butter is softened – about 30 seconds.

2 Make slightly diagonal cuts at 2 cm/ 1 inch intervals almost through to the base along the loaf and spread each side of these slices with the herb butter. Spread any leftover butter along the top and sides of the loaf.

3 Wrap the loaf in greaseproof paper or cling film and cook on HIGH for 1 minute 10 seconds. Unwrap and serve as an accompaniment to soups or salads.

Note: to crisp the top, place under a pre-heated hot grill for a few seconds before serving.

Variations
For a hot garlic loaf, mix 1-2 cloves garlic, finely chopped, into the softened butter.
For a hot anchovy loaf, beat ¼ teaspoon anchovy essence or a little anchovy paste to taste into the softened butter before spreading.
For a hot cinnamon loaf to serve with fruit soups or as a snack, use 1 teaspoon ground cinnamon and 1 teaspoon sugar instead of the herbs. Try using 2 Vienna loaves or some crusty brown rolls instead of the French loaf.

FISH AND SHELLFISH

It is almost worth owning a microwave cooker just to cook fish. The results are always successful as the fish stays moist and succulent and retains its fresh flavour. As the cooking time for most fish is so brief, take care not to over-cook, especially as the fish will continue to cook during the STANDING time.

When cooking whole fish remember to arrange them so that the thinner or small ends are positioned towards the centre of the microwave. When cooking a large fish, shield the thin part of the tail with foil to prevent over-cooking and prick the rest of the skin several times with the prongs of a fork to prevent it from bursting during the cooking process.

Hungarian scallops

Serves 6
40 g/1 ½ oz butter
1 small onion, chopped
100 g/4 oz frozen mixed diced peppers
2 tablespoons plain flour
4 teaspoons paprika
4 teaspoons lemon juice
225 g/8 oz frozen scallops, defrosted
150 ml/¼ pint water
2 teaspoons tomato purée
1 teaspoon salt
½ teaspoon pepper
4 medium tomatoes
4 tablespoons double cream

To garnish
piped creamed potatoes

1 Place butter in a large bowl and cook on HIGH for 45 seconds until melted.
2 Stir in the onion and peppers, cover with cling film and cook on HIGH for 2 minutes, then stir in the flour, paprika, lemon juice, scallops, water and tomato purée. Season with the salt and pepper and set aside.
3 Place the tomatoes in a bowl and cover with boiling water. Stand for 1 minute, then strip off the skins and cut out and discard the cores and seeds.
4 Roughly chop the tomato flesh and add this to the scallop mixture. Cover and cook on HIGH for 2 minutes, stir gently, then cook on HIGH for 2 minutes more. Stir in cream, and adjust the seasoning.
5 Serve in individual dishes, garnished with piped creamed potatoes. Brown briefly under a preheated hot grill.

Note: For attractive presentation serve this recipe in scrubbed scallop shells or ceramic shell-shaped dishes.

Variations
Top the mixture with breadcrumbs and Parmesan cheese before browning.
Replace the peppers and tomatoes with ½ teaspoon mustard powder for Devilled scallops.

Seafood brochettes with fennel rice (top, page 36) and Hungarian scallops.

Seafood brochettes with fennel rice

Serves 4
For the rice
225 g/8 oz easy-cook long grain rice
600 ml/1 pint boiling water
1 tablespoon oil
1½ teaspoons fennel seeds
1 teaspoon salt
For the brochettes
100 g/4 oz frozen scampi tails, defrosted
8 large frozen scallops, defrosted
225 g/8 oz frozen cod or haddock,
  defrosted and cut into bite-sized pieces
100 g/4 oz frozen whole mushrooms
1 red or green pepper, deseeded, cored
  and cut into 2.5 cm/1 inch pieces
For the sauce
50 g/2 oz butter
150 ml/¼ pint fish stock
1-2 tablespoons Pernod or Anise
142 ml/5 fl oz carton double cream
1 egg yolk
salt and pepper

1 For the rice: place the rice in a bowl and pour on the boiling water. Stir in the oil, fennel seeds and salt. Cover with cling film and cook on HIGH for 10 minutes. Leave to stand, covered, for a further 10 minutes.

2 For the brochettes: thread the scampi pieces, scallops, cod or haddock, mushrooms and pepper slices alternately on to *wooden* skewers. Place the brochettes in a shallow dish and cover with cling film. Cook on HIGH for 1½ minutes, then rearrange the brochettes in the dish. Re-cover and cook for a further 2 minutes. Pour off any cooking juices from the bottom of the dish and reserve in a medium-sized bowl.

3 For the sauce: add the butter to the reserved fish juices with the stock. Pour over the Pernod or Anise and cook on HIGH for 4 minutes. Blend the cream with the egg yolk and stir in the cream and season with salt and pepper. Cook for 2 minutes on HIGH, stirring after 1 minute, then stir and pour over the brochettes. Cover with cling film and cook for 1½ minutes. Allow to STAND, covered, for 2 minutes.

4 Spoon rice on to serving plates and arrange the brochettes across the rice. Spoon over the sauce. Or remove skewers before serving.

Poached cod with white wine sauce

Serves 4
8 × 75 g/3 oz frozen cod steaks, defrosted
150 ml/¼ pint dry white wine
salt and pepper
¼ red or green pepper, deseeded and cut
  into thin strips
For the sauce
1 tablespoon plain flour
1 tablespoon softened butter
a pinch of turmeric

1 Arrange the cod steaks in a single layer in a shallow dish. Pour over the wine and season lightly. Top each cod steak with strips of pepper.

2 Cover tightly with cling film and cook on HIGH for 5 minutes. Drain the cooking liquid into a jug.

3 For the sauce: beat the flour into the butter with the turmeric. Stir this into the cooking liquid to thicken it. Cook on HIGH for 1 minute. Stir well, then cook on HIGH for 1 minute, until thick.

4 Pour over the fish to serve.

Walnut-stuffed plaice

Serves 4
*8 frozen plaice fillets, skinned and
defrosted*
For the stuffing
50 g/2 oz butter
100 g/4 oz fresh wholemeal breadcrumbs
50 g/2 oz walnuts, finely chopped
25 g/1 oz watercress, finely chopped
*2 teaspoons chopped fresh sage leaves or
½ teaspoon dried sage*
*2 spring onions, white and green parts
trimmed and finely chopped*
½ teaspoon salt
freshly ground pepper
2 teaspoons lemon juice
1 egg, beaten

1 First make the stuffing: put 40 g/
1½ oz of the butter in a large bowl.
Cook on HIGH for 45 seconds until
melted.
2 Stir in the breadcrumbs, walnuts,
watercress, sage, spring onions and
salt and pepper and mix well. Add
the lemon juice and bind the
mixture with the beaten egg. It
should be fairly smooth.
3 Place the fish fillets with the
skinned sides facing up and spread
each one evenly with stuffing. Roll
up the fillet from the tail end and
secure in place with a wooden
cocktail stick.
4 Arrange the fish so they stand on
the rolled ends in a circle around
the edge of a buttered 1.2 litre/
2 pint deep, straight-sided dish.
Dot with the remaining butter.
5 Cover with cling film, puncture
the top, and cook on HIGH for
3 minutes. STAND for 2 minutes,
then serve with broccoli, leaf
spinach and sautéed potatoes or
a green salad.

Baked stuffed trout

Serves 2
*2 frozen rainbow trout, each weighing
about 250 g/9 oz, defrosted*
For the stuffing
2 rashers streaky bacon, rinds removed
2 tablespoons fresh white breadcrumbs
2 tablespoons finely chopped parsley
juice of one lemon
salt and pepper
To garnish
lemon slices and watercress sprigs

1 For the stuffing: place the bacon
rashers on a piece of absorbent
kitchen paper and cook, uncovered,
on HIGH for 30 seconds. Turn over
and cook on HIGH for a further 30
seconds, until cooked and crispy.
2 Mix together the breadcrumbs and
parsley. Moisten with a few drops
of the lemon juice. Crumble or
finely chop the bacon and add half
to the stuffing. Season lightly and
pack into the cavities in the trout.
3 Place the trout 'nose to tail' in a
shallow dish. Pour over the
remaining lemon juice, season with
salt and pepper and scatter over the
rest of the bacon. Cover with cling
film, puncture the top and cook on
HIGH for 5 minutes. Leave to
STAND for 3 minutes. Garnish with
lemon and watercress.

Variation
For lemon-stuffed trout with almonds,
place 3 lemon slices inside each fish.
Cover, puncture and cook as for
stuffed trout, then leave to STAND for
3 minutes. Cook 25 g/1 oz butter on
HIGH for 1 minute, then sprinkle with
a generous 25 g/1 oz flaked almonds.
Cook on HIGH for 2 minutes, until
lightly coloured. Sprinkle over the trout.

Fish and tomato lasagne

Serves 4-6

175 g/6 oz easy-cook green lasagne
For the sauce
600 ml/1 pint milk
25 g/1 oz frozen sliced carrot, or 1 carrot, sliced
1 stick celery, sliced
50 g/2 oz frozen sliced onion, or 1 small onion, sliced
4 parsley sprigs
strip of lemon rind
4 black peppercorns
50 g/2 oz butter
3 tablespoons plain flour
85 ml/3 fl oz dry white wine
salt and pepper
For the filling
100 g/4 oz frozen sliced onion, or 1 large onion, sliced
6 × 75 g/3 oz frozen cod steaks or fillets
1 tablespoon plain flour
150 ml/¼ pint fish stock
198 g/7 oz can tomatoes
2 tablespoons tomato purée
3 tablespoons chopped parsley
1 tablespoon lemon juice
75 g/3 oz mature Cheddar cheese, grated
cayenne pepper or nutmeg
For the topping
50 g/2 oz Parmesan cheese, grated

1 First make the sauce: Place milk in a large bowl with the carrot, celery, onion, parsley sprigs, lemon rind and peppercorns. Cook on HIGH for 6 minutes, or until the milk comes to the boil. Remove, cover and STAND for 15 minutes.
2 Place butter in a medium bowl and cook on HIGH for 1 minute until melted. Stir in flour and cook on HIGH for 1 minute. Gradually stir in the wine until smooth and set aside.
3 Strain the flavoured milk and gradually stir it into the blended wine, flour and butter mixture, until smooth. Cook on HIGH for 2 minutes. Remove, whisk well, then cook on HIGH for 1 minute. Remove, whisk again and cook on HIGH for 1 more minute, or until thickened. Adjust seasoning.
4 For the filling: place the onion and the fish in a shallow dish, cover with cling film, puncture the top, and cook on HIGH for 6 minutes. Test the fish with a fork to see if it flakes easily. If it does, it is cooked. Flake the fish.
5 Blend the flour with a little of the stock, then stir in the remaining stock, tomatoes, tomato purée, parsley, and season with salt, pepper and lemon juice.
6 Lightly grease a 2 litre/3½ pint shallow ovenproof dish. Lay one third of the pasta in the dish and cover with half the fish mixture. Spoon one third of the sauce over the fish and sprinkle with half the grated Cheddar cheese. Sprinkle lightly with cayenne pepper or nutmeg. Repeat the layers (lasagne/fish mixture/sauce/cheese and cayenne or nutmeg) and cover top with remaining lasagne and sauce.
7 Cover with cling film, puncture the top and cook on HIGH for 8 minutes. Leave to STAND for 10 minutes.
8 For the topping, sprinkle the Parmesan cheese evenly over the top and flash under a pre-heated medium grill for up to 5 minutes to brown the top. Serve with a salad, or cooked green beans, courgettes or spinach.

Fish and tomato lasagne.

MEAT AND POULTRY

Cooking meat in the microwave cooker reduces cooking times by about one third and brings out the fullest flavour by preserving most of the natural juices. As with all meat cookery the end result will depend on the quality of the meat used. But good results using tougher cuts can easily be achieved by cooking the meat on a low power setting, for a longer period of time – and by braising these cuts of meat in liquid such as stock or wine or by marinating them beforehand. Casserole dishes are more tender and tastier if allowed to cool slowly after cooking; then reheat them gently before serving.

Contrary to popular belief, most meat will colour when cooked in the microwave cooker. Large joints will brown because of their fat content and the longer cooking time involved. But smaller cuts such as chops may need a little help from a special microwave browning dish (see page 9), and some microwave seasoning which will add colour as well as flavour.

Poultry cooked in the microwave stays plump and succulent and hardly shrinks at all. It is especially delicious if the skin has been flavoured with a seasoning such as cumin, coriander, paprika, chopped herbs and crushed garlic. Rub seasonings of your choice over the skin before cooking as this will also help colour the roast.

Spiced beef

Serves 4

25 g/1 oz butter
100 g/4 oz frozen sliced carrots, or 2 carrots, sliced
75 g/3 oz frozen sliced onion, or 1 onion, sliced
1 kg/2 lb boned, rolled brisket of beef

For the marinade

150 ml/¼ pint olive oil
150 ml/¼ pint red wine
2 tablespoons red wine vinegar
2 tablespoons brown sugar
a pinch each of ground cloves, mixed spice, allspice, cinnamon and nutmeg plus 2 whole cloves
a pinch of chopped fresh thyme or dried thyme
½ teaspoon each, salt and freshly ground black pepper

1 Place the butter in a 1.75 litre/3 pint deep casserole dish and cook on HIGH for 30 seconds until melted. Stir in the carrots and onion and cook on HIGH for 3 minutes.

2 Mix together the marinade ingredients and heat on HIGH for 1 minute.

3 Place the beef on top of the vegetables in the dish and pour the marinade over. Add cold water to cover. Cover with cling film and leave to marinate overnight. Puncture the top of the cling film and cook on HIGH for 20 minutes. Leave to STAND in the dish until cold.

4 Drain the meat and place in a bowl. Cover with a plate and add weights (cans of food are ideal). Press and chill for 24 hours before slicing.

Shepherd's pie

Serves 4-6

For the topping
1 kg/2 lb potatoes, peeled and cubed
3 tablespoons water
1 egg, beaten
15 g/½ oz butter
salt and pepper
a sprinkling of paprika (optional)

For the pie
75 g/3 oz frozen sliced onion, or 1 onion,
   chopped
700 g/1½ lb frozen free-flow minced beef
2 tablespoons tomato purée
1 teaspoon dried mixed herbs
a few drops of Worcestershire sauce
1 celery stick, chopped
100 g/4 oz frozen sliced mushrooms
salt and pepper

1 For the topping: put the potatoes in a large bowl with the water. Cover with cling film, puncture the top and cook on HIGH for 6 minutes. Stir, then cook on HIGH for 6 minutes. Set aside to STAND.
2 For the pie: spread the onion over the base of a large casserole and cover with cling film. Puncture the top. Cook on HIGH for 4 minutes.
3 Add the beef to the onion, cover and cook on HIGH for 6 minutes, stirring three times during cooking. Pour off excess liquid.
4 Add the rest of the ingredients and season to taste. Cover and cook on HIGH for 9 minutes, stirring once during cooking.
5 Drain and mash the potatoes with the egg and butter. Season with salt and pepper and pipe or spread over the mixture. Cook, uncovered, for a further 4 minutes on HIGH.
6 Sprinkle with a little paprika or brown under a conventional grill.

Cannelloni al sugo

Serves 4

8 green cannelloni tubes

For the filling
100 g/4 oz frozen sliced onions
1 garlic clove, crushed with a little salt
½ teaspoon dried basil
½ teaspoon dried oregano
225 g/8 oz frozen free-flow minced beef
2 tablespoons tomato purée
salt and pepper

For the sauce
600 ml/1 pint Basic white sauce (page 58)
100 g/4 oz frozen sliced mushrooms
50 g/2 oz mature Cheddar cheese, grated
1 teaspoon lemon juice

To garnish
1 tablespoon grated Parmesan cheese
2 tablespoons chopped parsley

1 For the filling: place the onion in a bowl with the garlic and herbs. Cover and cook on HIGH for 5 minutes.
2 Add the meat and tomato purée, stirring to mix. Season with salt and pepper. Cover with cling film, puncture the top and cook on HIGH for 3 minutes. Stir well, cover and cook on HIGH for 3 minutes. Set aside.
3 Make the Basic white sauce. Add mushrooms, cheese and lemon juice, stir well then set aside.
4 Using a teaspoon, carefully fill the cannelloni tubes with the filling. Arrange them in a single layer in a shallow 1.2 litre/2 pint capacity dish.
5 Pour over the sauce. Cover with cling film, puncture the top and cook on HIGH for 14 minutes. STAND for about 4 minutes. Sprinkle with Parmesan and parsley and serve.

Beef and chestnut casserole

Serves 6

175 g/6 oz frozen onion slices, or 2 onions,
* sliced*
175 g/6 oz frozen sliced carrots, or 3
* medium carrots, peeled and sliced*
2 tablespoons oil
2 tablespoons flour
1 beef stock cube, crumbled
300 ml/½ pint boiling water
1 kg/2 lb good-quality braising steak,
* cubed*
300 ml/½ pint dark ale or beer
425 g/15 oz can whole peeled chestnuts,
* drained*
2 teaspoons French wholegrain mustard
2 teaspoons soy sauce
175 g/6 oz frozen whole mushrooms, or
* the equivalent quantity of fresh*
* mushrooms, wiped*
salt and pepper

Beef and chestnut casserole.

1 Place the onion in a large casserole with the carrots and oil. Cook on HIGH for 4 minutes, then stir in the flour.
2 Dissolve the stock cubes in the boiling water and stir into the vegetables. Add the meat, beer, chestnuts, mustard and soy sauce, and stir well.
3 Cover with cling film, puncture the top and cook on LOW for 20 minutes. Stir and cook on LOW for a further 20 minutes.
4 Add the mushrooms and cook on LOW for 20 minutes. Test the meat, adjust the seasoning, if necessary, and continue cooking on DEFROST for 10 minutes. STAND for 5-10 minutes before serving.

Notes: This casserole is even better when cooked in advance and reheated.

If using cubed stewing steak, cook the meat and vegetables on HIGH for 5 minutes, then continue cooking from stage 2 at SIMMER for about 1½ hours. Check and stir regularly during cooking.

Variations

For a beef and chestnut pie, add a topping of creamed potato, sprinkle with grated cheese and finish under a pre-heated hot grill. Or cook in a 1½ litre/2½ pint pie dish and roll out a round of shortcrust pastry to fit the top. Cut 2 slits to allow steam to escape and finish by baking in a conventional oven.

Try replacing the whole chestnuts and French mustard with 175 g/6 oz stoned black olives and 1 teaspoon of anchovy essence, and the beer with a robust red wine, for a beef and olive casserole.

Hurry curry

Serves 4

1 tablespoon oil
100 g/4 oz frozen mixed diced peppers, or
1 large green pepper, cored, deseeded
and sliced
100 g/4 oz frozen sliced onion, or 1 large
onion, sliced
2 garlic cloves, crushed with a little salt
1 teaspoon turmeric
1 teaspoon salt
1½ teaspoons curry powder, or to taste
1 teaspoon ground ginger
a pinch of chili powder
500 g/1 lb frozen free-flow minced beef
2 tablespoons flour
4 tomatoes, skinned and chopped
2 teaspoons tomato purée
300 ml/½ pint beef stock

1   Place the oil in a bowl with the pepper, onion, garlic and the turmeric. Add the salt, curry powder, ginger and chili powder.

2   Cover with cling film and puncture. Cook on HIGH for 3 minutes.

3   Toss the minced meat in the flour, then add to the vegetables and spices. Stir and mix well. Cover, puncture the top and cook on HIGH for 10 minutes. Then stir again, re-cover and cook on MEDIUM for 10 minutes.

4   Add the tomatoes, tomato purée and stock. Stir, re-cover and cook on MEDIUM for 10 minutes. Check for readiness and thicken the curry, if necessary, with a little extra flour mixed to a paste with a little cold water. Cover and cook on MEDIUM for 2 minutes. STAND for 5 minutes.

5   Serve with boiled rice, poppadums and mango chutney. To cook poppadums: place 3 at a time in the cooker and heat on HIGH for 1 minute, turning halfway.

Hurry curry (left) and Pork succotash (page 44).

Pork succotash

Serves 4-6

500 g/1 lb frozen diced pork, defrosted
2 tablespoons oil
75 g/3 oz small sweet pickled onions
1 teaspoon green peppercorns
175 g/6 oz frozen cut green beans
225 g/8 oz frozen broad beans
225 g/8 oz frozen sweetcorn
salt and pepper
2 bay leaves, crushed
3 tablespoons plain flour
¼ teaspoon ground cloves
150 ml/¼ pint chicken stock
4 tablespoons double cream

1 Heat a browning dish for 5-8 minutes, or according to the manufacturer's instructions and use to sear the pork, or quickly fry it in a heavy-based frying pan in a little extra fat, if necessary, to brown it a little.

2 Place the oil in a large bowl, cover with cling film and cook on HIGH for 1½ minutes. Add meat, turn it in the oil, then add the onions, peppercorns, two kinds of bean and sweetcorn, and stir well.

3 Cover with cling film and cook on HIGH for 8 minutes. Stir in the salt, pepper, bay leaves, flour, ground cloves and stock and mix well. Cook, uncovered, on HIGH for 4 minutes.

4 Stir in the cream, adjust the seasoning and cook on HIGH for 4 minutes. STAND for 5 minutes, then serve with creamy mashed potatoes, browned under a grill.

Variation
If green peppercorns are unavailable use capers along with a little of their vinegar.

Stuffed pork chops 'au four'

Serves 4

500 g/1 lb even-sized potatoes
4 large frozen pork loin chops, defrosted
397 g/14 oz can chopped tomatoes
salt and pepper
For the stuffing
4 tablespoons sage and onion stuffing mix
3-4 tablespoons boiling water
a knob of butter
½ stick celery, finely chopped
2 tablespoons grated cheese

1 Grease an oval gratin dish large enough to take the chops comfortably. Set aside.

2 Wipe the potatoes and place them, in their jackets, evenly spaced in a ring around the edge of the turntable or on a dish. Cover with cling film, puncture and cook on HIGH for 8-10 minutes, until cooked but still easy to slice.

3 For the stuffing: mix the sage and onion stuffing mix with the water and a little butter. Beat in the celery and cheese.

4 Slit the chops along the side opposite the bone, making a good 7.5 cm/3 inch slit. Work the knife through to the bone to make a pocket. Divide the stuffing between the chops, close and secure with wooden cocktail sticks.

5 Peel and slice potatoes and arrange over the base of the gratin dish. Arrange the pork chops over the potatoes and pour over the tomatoes with their juice. Season lightly with salt and pepper, cover with cling film and puncture the top. Cook on HIGH for 12 minutes.

6 Test and cook for a further 2 minutes on HIGH, if necessary.

Sweet and sour lamb

Serves 4

*500 g/1 lb lamb neck fillet, thinly
   sliced*
2 tablespoons olive oil
1 teaspoon sesame seeds
*75 g/3 oz frozen sliced onion, or
   1 onion, sliced*
2 sticks celery, sliced
2 carrots, peeled and cut into sticks
50 g/2 oz frozen mixed diced peppers
225 g/8 oz canned pineapple chunks
3 tablespoons cornflour
3 tablespoons orange juice
2 tablespoons lemon juice
2 tablespoons tomato ketchup
1 tablespoon soy sauce
*100 g/4 oz frozen button mushrooms,
   quartered*
salt and pepper
¼ teaspoon ground allspice

1 Dry-fry or grill the lamb just to
   slightly brown the meat or use a
   browning dish (see the recipe for
   Pork succotash). Set aside.
2 Place the oil and sesame seeds in a
   large bowl. Cover with cling film
   and cook on HIGH for 1½ minutes.
   Add meat and cook for 1½ minutes
   on HIGH.
3 Stir in onion, celery, carrots and the
   mixed diced peppers. Drain the
   pineapple, reserving the juice. Add
   the pineapple to the mixture.
4 Blend the cornflour with the
   reserved pineapple juice, orange
   and lemon juices, ketchup and soy
   sauce. Stir into the meat and
   vegetables and mix well. Cook on
   HIGH for 6 minutes. Stir.
5 Add the mushrooms, season to
   taste and mix in the allspice. Cook
   on HIGH for 5 minutes. Stir, then
   STAND for 5 minutes.

Somerset liver

Serves 4

*350 g/12 oz frozen lamb's liver, thinly
   sliced and defrosted*
50 g/2 oz butter
*100 g/4 oz frozen sliced onion, or 1 large
   onion, sliced*
175 g/6 oz frozen apple slices
2 teaspoons lemon juice
3 tablespoons plain flour
150 ml/¼ pint cider
3 tablespoons whisky (optional)
salt and pepper
*1 tablespoon chopped fresh sage or 1
   teaspoon dried sage*
142 ml/5 fl oz carton double cream
To garnish
sage leaves or 25 g/1 oz toasted almonds

1 Heat a browning dish for 5-8
   minutes, or according to the
   manufacturer's instructions and use
   to sear the liver lightly. Set aside.
2 Place the butter in a large shallow
   dish and then cook it on HIGH for
   1 minute 10 seconds until melted.
3 Add the onion, apple slices and
   lemon juice, cover with cling film
   and cook on HIGH for 6 minutes.
   Uncover and stir well to break the
   apple down to a purée.
4 Stir in the flour, then gradually stir
   in the cider and the whisky, if using.
   Season with salt and pepper and
   add the sage and liver slices.
5 Cook on HIGH for 3 minutes. Stir.
   Stir in the cream and cook on HIGH
   for a further 3 minutes. Stir again,
   then STAND for 4 minutes.
6 Serve garnished with sage leaves or
   toasted almonds.

Note: To remove strong flavours from
liver, soak in milk for up to one hour
before cooking.

Country veal casserole

Serves 4-6

2 × 397 g/14 oz packs of frozen diced
veal, defrosted, or 750 g/1¾ lb pie veal,
trimmed and diced
2 tablespoons mixed chopped fresh herbs,
or 1 tablespoon mixed dried herbs
175 g/6 oz frozen sliced onion, or 2
medium onions, sliced
2 tablespoons oil
3 tablespoons plain flour
250 ml/8 fl oz dry white wine
1 chicken stock cube
500 g/1 lb frozen farmhouse-style
vegetable mix, or 500 g/1 lb mixed fresh
vegetables (cauliflower, French beans,
carrots), trimmed and sliced, and a
handful of frozen peas
salt and pepper
142 ml/5 fl oz carton double cream
1 teaspoon lemon juice

1 Mix together the veal, herbs, onion
and oil in a large bowl. Stir to mix
well.
2 Cover with cling film and cook on
HIGH for 5 minutes.
3 Stir in the flour and wine, and
crumble in the stock cube. Add the
mixed vegetables and stir well to
combine thoroughly.
4 Cover again and cook on HIGH for
4 minutes. Stir in salt and pepper to
taste and the cream and lemon
juice.
5 Cover again and cook on MEDIUM
for 6 minutes. Do not allow to boil.
STAND for about 1 minute before
serving with baked potatoes and a
fresh green salad.

Variation

This recipe works well with turkey, in
addition add 100 g/4 oz diced cooked
ham or lean bacon.

Breast of lamb with apricot stuffing

Serves 2-3

1 boned breast of lamb, weighing about
500 g/1 lb

For the stuffing

2 tablespoons oil
100 g/4 oz dried apricots, roughly
chopped
50 g/2 oz walnuts, finely chopped
50 g/2 oz fresh white breadcrumbs
50 g/2 oz sultanas
salt and pepper
1 teaspoon ground cumin
1 egg, beaten

1 Heat the oil in a bowl for 1 minute
on HIGH. Stir in the apricots,
walnuts, breadcrumbs, and
sultanas. Season with salt, pepper
and half the cumin and bind with
the beaten egg.
2 Spoon the stuffing evenly over the
boned breast of lamb. Roll-up and
tie firmly in three places with string,
packing in any extra stuffing.
3 Rub the remaining cumin over the
lamb and place the roll in a shallow
dish. Cook, uncovered, on HIGH for
4 minutes. Turn meat over and
cook on HIGH for 4-5 minutes.
4 Remove from the cooker, wrap in
foil and STAND for at least 10
minutes. Serve with a selection of
boiled vegetables.

Note: to serve 4-6, double the
quantity of stuffing and use to fill two
equal-size lamb breasts, separately
rolled. Cook 7 minutes each side – but
keep testing. STAND, wrapped in foil,
for 10 minutes.

*Country veal casserole (top) and Breast of
lamb with apricot stuffing.*

Roast chicken with pâté stuffing

Serves 6-8
1.5 kg/3¼ lb frozen roasting chicken, defrosted
salt and pepper
For the stuffing
25 g/1 oz butter
liver from the chicken, finely chopped
100 g/4 oz smooth liver or pork pâté
50 g/2 oz fresh white breadcrumbs
1 tablespoon sherry or brandy

1 For the stuffing: place the butter in a bowl and cook on HIGH for 1 minute until melted. Stir in the chicken liver, cover with cling film, puncture the top and cook on HIGH for 30-45 seconds.
2 Mix in the pâté and breadcrumbs, stir in the sherry or brandy and add salt and pepper to taste.
3 Pat the chicken dry with absorbent kitchen paper. Season the insides of the chicken with salt and pepper. Lift the skin in front of the breast flap and with the fingers of the other hand, carefully make a wide pocket between the flesh and skin by working the chicken skin loose over both sides of the breast, going as far down to the 'tail' as possible without breaking the skin.
4 Spread the stuffing evenly under skin. And secure the skin in place with wooden cocktail sticks.
5 Either place the bird in a shallow dish, tying the ends of the legs close to the body and covering loosely with cling film, or place inside a roasting bag, tie the end loosely with string and puncture the bag with a sharp knife.
6 Cook on HIGH for 23 minutes, then leave to STAND for 15-20 minutes.

Chicken flamenco

Serves 4
2 tablespoons olive oil
4 frozen chicken joints, defrosted
100 g/4 oz frozen sliced onion, or 1 large onion, sliced
100 g/4 oz frozen mixed diced peppers
198 g/7 oz can tomatoes, drained
50 g/2 oz stuffed green olives
2 cloves garlic, peeled and crushed
2 tablespoons tomato purée
300 ml/½ pint chicken stock
1 teaspoon dried mixed herbs
dash of Tabasco sauce
salt and pepper
2 tablespoons cornflour
2 tablespoons dry sherry

1 Pour oil into a large casserole dish, cover and cook on HIGH for 1½ minutes. Add chicken portions, skin side down. Cover with cling film, puncture the top and cook on HIGH for 3 minutes. Remove the chicken pieces and set aside.
2 Add the onion, peppers, tomatoes, olives, garlic and tomato purée to oil in casserole and mix well. Cook on HIGH for 2 minutes, then stir in the stock, herbs and Tabasco and season to taste.
3 Replace chicken portions in the casserole, making sure they are covered by sauce. Cover with cling film and cook on HIGH for 5 minutes.
4 Turn and rearrange the chicken portions in the dish to ensure even cooking. Cook on HIGH for a further 5 minutes.
5 Blend the cornflour with the sherry until smooth and stir into the casserole. Cook on HIGH for 4 minutes. Stir and allow to STAND for 5 minutes before serving.

Marinated poussins with tarragon sauce

Serves 2

2 frozen poussins, or spring chickens, defrosted
2 tablespoons oil
For the marinade
4 tablespoons dry white wine
2 tablespoons white wine vinegar
3 tablespoons olive oil
1 teaspoon caster sugar
1 teaspoon lemon juice
1 teaspoon grated lemon rind (optional)
For the sauce
40 g/1 ½ oz butter
40 g/1 ½ oz plain flour
300 ml/½ pint milk
150 ml/¼ pint dry white wine
2 tablespoons chopped fresh tarragon or 2 teaspoons dried tarragon
salt and pepper
To garnish
fresh tarragon sprigs

1   Split the poussins in half lengthways. Mix together the marinade ingredients, pour over poussins and leave for 2-4 hours. Drain birds, reserving marinade.
2   Heat the oil in a frying pan and quickly brown the birds on all sides. Place in a casserole, add marinade, cover with cling film and cook on HIGH for 12 minutes. Set aside.
3   For the sauce: place the butter in a bowl and cook on HIGH for 10 seconds, until melted. Stir in the flour to make a smooth paste and set aside. Pour the milk into a jug with the wine and the cooking juices from the birds. Cook on HIGH for 4 minutes. Stir into the flour mixture and cook on HIGH for 2 minutes. Stir in tarragon and cook on HIGH for 2 minutes. Season.
4   Arrange the poussins on a serving dish, cover with the sauce and garnish with fresh tarragon.

Variations
Use chicken portions instead of poussins. Omit the vinegar and lemon juice from the marinade and substitute 3 tablespoons brandy and 1 teaspoon ground coriander.

Chicken escalopes à la suisse

Serves 2

2 frozen chicken breast portions, defrosted and boned
50 g/2 oz butter
50 g/2 oz smoked Continental ham (such as Prosciutto)
25 g/1 oz Gruyère cheese, grated
salt and pepper
To garnish
2 tablespoons chopped parsley

1   Place each of the chicken breasts between 2 sheets of greaseproof paper and beat with a rolling pin to flatten them as thinly as possible. Place on a micro-proof plate.
2   Dot with the butter, cover tightly with cling film and cook on HIGH for 3 minutes.
3   Arrange the slices of ham in folds on the chicken escalopes and sprinkle with the grated cheese. Season generously.
4   Cook, uncovered, on HIGH for 3 minutes. Garnish with parsley and serve with sweetcorn and broccoli.

Variation
Marinate the chicken before cooking for up to one hour, in 3 tablespoons sherry and 2 tablespoons soy sauce.

Marinated poussins with tarragon sauce (page 49).

▌Mediterranean grill

Serves 4

100 g/4 oz frozen diced chicken, defrosted
8 bay leaves
8 frozen cocktail sausages, defrosted, and
* skins pricked*
2 tomatoes, quartered
4 button onions, peeled
For the marinade
3 tablespoons olive oil
3 tablespoons dry white wine
2 teaspoons lemon juice
salt and pepper
½ teaspoon dried rosemary
½ teaspoon dried thyme
1 clove garlic, crushed with a little salt
For the meatballs
175 g/6 oz frozen minced beef, defrosted
1 tablespoon plain flour
½ teaspoon ground cumin
½ teaspoon ground coriander
1 egg
salt and pepper

1 For the marinade: mix together all the marinade ingredients. Place the chicken pieces, bay leaves and sausages in a bowl and pour over the marinade.
2 For the meatballs: place all the ingredients in a bowl, blender or food processor and mix or process until very smooth, or evenly mixed. With floured hands, pinch off walnut-sized pieces of the mixture and roll them into balls. Add them to the marinade as you make them, continuing until all the mixture is used up. Turn them carefully in the marinade, then leave to stand for 20 minutes.
3 Thread wooden skewers alternately with chicken cubes, bay leaves, sausages, tomato wedges, meatballs and button onions. Brush each skewer with the marinade and arrange in a shallow dish.
4 Cover with cling film and cook on HIGH for 8 minutes.
5 Pre-heat the grill to hot and brown the kebabs for up to 5 minutes. Serve on a bed of green salad with lemon wedges.

Variations
Make the meatballs from ground lamb for an even more authentic flavour of the Middle East – try a marinade using ½ teaspoon chopped fresh green chili pepper, some finely chopped fresh ginger and yoghurt in place of the herbs, oil and wine. Garnish with mint.
   Instead of cocktail sausages try a spicy salami cut into thick cubes.
   For an oriental flavour, replace the herbs in the marinade with sliced root ginger, coriander and turmeric. Perhaps even use coconut milk instead of the oil and wine.

Quick cassoulet

Serves 4-6

50 g/2 oz butter
3-4 garlic cloves, crushed
100 g/4 oz frozen sliced onion, or 1 large onion, sliced
100 g/4 oz streaky bacon or bacon pieces, rinds removed and chopped
3 tablespoons chopped fresh parsley
2 tablespoons plain flour
½ teaspoon dried mixed herbs
1 tablespoon wholegrain mustard
150 ml/¼ pint chicken stock
397 g/14 oz can tomatoes
397 g/14 oz can red kidney beans, drained
397 g/14 oz can butter beans, drained
salt and black pepper
4 herb pork or pork and beef sausages, halved
1 tablespoon sherry
100 g/4 oz fresh wholemeal breadcrumbs
50 g/2 oz mature Cheddar cheese, grated

1 Place butter in a 1.75 litre/3 pint deep casserole dish and cook on HIGH for 1 minute until melted.

2 Stir in the garlic, onion and bacon, and cook on HIGH for 3 minutes.

3 Stir in the parsley, flour, herbs and mustard, then add the stock, tomatoes and two kinds of beans and mix well. Season lightly.

4 Add the sausages, cover with cling film, puncture the top and cook on HIGH for 10 minutes. Stir in the sherry, then cook on HIGH for a further 2 minutes.

5 Mix together the breadcrumbs and cheese and sprinkle the mixture over the top in an even layer and brown under a preheated hot grill for up to 5 minutes, so a crust forms. Serve with grilled or baked tomatoes.

Variations

Use Continental sausages, such as Italian sweet sausages or frankfurters, instead of herb pork sausages. Serve with a green salad.

Quick cassoulet (left) and Mediterranean grill.

VEGETABLES

Not only do vegetables retain more flavour when cooked in the microwave cooker, but they keep their shape and colour perfectly and do not lose much of their valuable vitamin content. This is due to the speed at which they cook and the fact that very little water is needed during cooking.

For best results, cook vegetables in a dish covered with cling film or in a boiling bag or 'roaster' bag, sealed loosely with string or an elastic band.

Always remember that vegetables should only be cooked until *almost* tender, as they continue cooking during standing time.

Swiss cheese pudding with vegetables

Serves 6
For the base
50 g/2 oz butter
25 g/1 oz Gruyère cheese, grated
75 g/3 oz frozen sliced onion, or 1 onion, chopped
225 g/8 oz frozen broccoli, defrosted and roughly chopped
100 g/4 oz frozen cauliflower florets
25 g/1 oz ground almonds
4 tablespoons dry white wine
salt and pepper
For the topping
300 ml/½ pint milk
50 g/2 oz butter
50 g/2 oz plain flour
4 eggs, separated
1 tablespoon wholegrain mustard
150 g/5 oz Gruyère cheese, finely grated
¼ teaspoon ground nutmeg
To serve
soured cream

1 Use the butter to grease the insides of a 2 litre/3½ pint soufflé dish, then sprinkle thickly with the grated cheese. Tap out excess.

2 Place the onion, broccoli and cauliflower in a bowl, cover with cling film and cook on HIGH for 3 minutes. Spoon the vegetables into the prepared soufflé dish and smooth the top.

3 Sprinkle in the almonds, wine, salt and pepper.

4 For the topping: pour the milk into a large jug and cook on HIGH for 3 minutes to heat. Place butter in a bowl and cook on HIGH for 1 minute until melted.

5 Stir the flour into the melted butter and beat well. Gradually stir in the hot milk, whisking until smooth. Cook on HIGH For 1½ minutes. Whisk, then return to the cooker and cook for a further 1 minute.

6 Whisk in the egg yolks, mustard, salt and pepper. Beat in the Gruyère cheese. Whisk the egg whites until stiff and carefully fold into the sauce mixture.

7 Turn the mixture into the soufflé dish over the vegetables and sprinkle with a little nutmeg. Cook on HIGH for 7 minutes. Serve immediately with a little soured cream poured over the top.

Green beans with almonds

Serves 4
500 g/1 lb frozen whole green beans
50 g/2 oz butter
salt and pepper
50 g/2 oz flaked almonds

1 Place the green beans in a bowl and add 2 tablespoons water. Cover with cling film, puncture the top and cook on HIGH for 5 minutes. Remove from the cooker, stir, cover and cook on HIGH for a further 5 minutes. STAND for 3 minutes, covered. Season to taste.
2 Place the butter in a bowl with the almonds and cook on HIGH for 3 minutes, until the butter is melted and the almonds are lightly coloured.
3 Stir the almonds into the beans before serving.

Stuffed tomatoes

Serves 4
1 tablespoon olive oil
100 g/4 oz fresh wholemeal breadcrumbs
100 g/4 oz frozen sliced mushrooms
75 g/3 oz frozen sliced onion, or 1 onion, finely chopped
50 g/2 oz frozen pork sausagemeat, defrosted
1 teaspoon dill seeds
2 spring onions, trimmed and finely chopped
75 g/3 oz hazelnuts, finely chopped
salt and pepper
4 large 'beef' tomatoes, wiped

1 Place all the ingredients except the tomatoes in a large bowl and mix.
2 Cook on HIGH for 2 minutes.

3 Slice the tops off the tomatoes and set aside. Scoop out the flesh, discard the seeds and chop the flesh. Stir this into the stuffing mixture.
4 Fill the tomatoes, replace the tops and cook on HIGH for 3-4 minutes. STAND for 2 minutes.

Barbecued corn cobs

Serves 2
2 frozen corn cobs
40 g/1 ½ oz butter
2 tablespoons tomato ketchup
a few drops of Worcestershire sauce

1 Place the butter in a bowl and cook on HIGH for 1 ½ minutes, then beat in the tomato ketchup and flavour to taste with Worcestershire sauce.
2 Place the corn on an ovenproof plate and cook on HIGH for 4 minutes. Remove and place each cob on a large piece of greaseproof paper. Pour the sauce over each cob and folding up the ends of the greaseproof paper seal them to form a parcel.
3 Cook on HIGH for a further 4 minutes then STAND for 2 minutes. Serve in the parcels.

Note: For fresh corn cobs, allow 2 minutes less per side. Test after 4 minutes – overcooking may toughen the skins.

Variation
For Devilled corn cobs, add about 2 tablespoons of honey, 1 tablespoon of fresh chopped basil (or 1 teaspoon of dried basil) and a few drops of Tabasco or a pinch of chili powder to the basic barbecue sauce.

Parsnip croquettes

Makes 12
700 g/1 ½ lb frozen parsnips
1 tablespoon lemon juice
300 ml/½ pint boiling water
½ (131 g/4 oz) packet of instant potato
  granules
1 egg
50 g/2 oz butter
salt and pepper
¼ teaspoon ground nutmeg
a little milk, if necessary
For the coating
1 egg, beaten
142 g/5 oz packet golden breadcrumbs

1 Place parsnips in a bowl, add the lemon juice and boiling water. Cover, puncture the top and cook on HIGH for 8 minutes until tender. STAND for 5 minutes.
2 Empty the potato granules into a bowl and use the water from the cooked parsnips to reconstitute the potato. Add the egg, butter, salt and pepper and the nutmeg. Add milk, if needed, then mix well.
3 Mash the parsnips until smooth and beat into the potato mixture. Chill until firm, about 20 minutes. Roll the mixture into balls or the traditional 'cork' shapes.
4 Dip first into the beaten egg and then into the crumbs until each croquette is evenly coated. Arrange on a plate and cook on HIGH for 4 minutes before serving.

Lemon-glazed carrots

Serves 4
500 g/1 lb frozen sliced carrots
3 tablespoons soft brown sugar
3 tablespoons lemon juice
grated rind of 1 lemon

1 Place all the ingredients together in a casserole dish. Cover with cling film, puncture the top and cook on HIGH for 15 minutes.
2 STAND, covered, for 5 minutes before serving.

Lemon-glazed carrots (left) and Parsnip croquettes.

Old-fashioned potato cake

Serves 6

15 g/½ oz butter
1 kg/2 lb waxy potatoes (e.g. King
  Edwards), thinly sliced
100 g/4 oz Red Leicester, Double
  Gloucester or Cheddar cheese, grated
salt and pepper
ground nutmeg
150 ml/¼ pint milk
snipped chives to garnish

1 Place the butter in a 20 cm/8 inch shallow baking dish. Cook on HIGH for 20 seconds until melted, then tip dish to coat base and sides.
2 Place a layer of potato slices over the bottom of the dish, sprinkle with some of the cheese and season lightly with salt, pepper and a sprinkling of nutmeg. Repeat the layers until the dish is full, pour on the milk and finish with a layer of cheese.
3 Cover with cling film, puncture the top and cook on HIGH for 15 minutes. Test with a skewer and continue cooking on HIGH for a further 15-20 minutes, until the potatoes are cooked. STAND for 3 minutes before serving, garnish with chives.

Note: the exact cooking time depends on the type of potato and the thinness of the slices.

Variation
Mix two cloves garlic, lightly crushed with a little salt, into the cheese before sprinkling and omit the nutmeg.

Old-fashioned potato cake (top) and Broccoli cheese (page 56).

Broccoli cheese

Serves 4
500 g/1 lb frozen broccoli florets
2-4 tablespoons water
salt and pepper
80 g/2¾ oz packet cream cheese with
  garlic and herbs

1 Put 2 tablespoons water in the base of a round shallow dish and add a little salt. Arrange the broccoli around the sides in a circle and cook, uncovered, on HIGH for 6 minutes.
2 Crumble the garlic cheese over the broccoli, add a little extra water if necessary. Cover, puncture the top and cook on HIGH for 2 minutes. Check for readiness and seasoning. STAND for 2 minutes before serving.

Crunchy cabbage medley

Serves 4
500 g/1 lb white cabbage, finely
  shredded
175 g/6 oz frozen sliced onion, or 1 large
  onion, thinly sliced
1 medium carrot, grated
salt and pepper
¼ teaspoon mace
½ teaspoon dried mixed herbs or dried
  thyme
25 g/1 oz butter

1 Spread the cabbage in a layer over the base of a shallow dish. Sprinkle over the onion, followed by the carrot. Season lightly with salt and pepper and add the mace and the dried mixed herbs or the dried thyme.

2 Cover with cling film, puncture the top and cook on HIGH for 5 minutes. Fork through the layers to mix them together, cover again and cook on HIGH for 5 minutes.
3 Remove the covering, fork again to mix, dot the top with butter and cook, uncovered, on HIGH for 3-4 minutes. Adjust the seasoning. Serve with roast meat or poultry.

'Heaven and Earth'

Serves 4
3 large even-sized potatoes
500 g/1 lb frozen apple slices
100 g/4 oz frozen sliced onion, or 1
  medium onion, sliced
25 g/1 oz dripping or butter
salt and pepper

1 Wipe the potatoes and prick the skins in several places. Arrange them spaced around the edge of the turntable and cook on HIGH for 7 minutes. Turn upside-down and continue cooking on HIGH for 7 minutes, or until cooked. Set aside.
2 Place the apple slices in a bowl and cook on HIGH for 2-3 minutes, or until soft.
3 Place the onion in a bowl with the dripping or butter and cook on HIGH for 3 minutes, then stir and cook on HIGH for 3 minutes.
4 Meanwhile, scrape the potato flesh into a bowl, discarding the skins. Add the cooked apple and mash together until smooth. Season with salt and pepper and serve with a layer of cooked onion slices on top.

Note: This dish is delicious with all types of rich meat dishes and goes particularly well with continental or traditional sausages.

Layered vegetable pie

Serves 8

2 large onions, thinly sliced
500 g/1 lb frozen sliced carrots
3 celery sticks, trimmed and sliced
25 g/1 oz butter
500 g/1 lb frozen cauliflower florets
225 g/8 oz frozen mushrooms
600 ml/1 pint Basic white sauce (page 58)
75 g/3 oz Cheddar cheese, grated
For the potato purée topping
500 g/1 lb even-sized potatoes
25 g/1 oz butter
4 tablespoons milk
salt and pepper

1 For the potato purée topping: wipe the potatoes and place them, in their jackets, evenly spaced in a ring around the edge of the turntable or dish. Cover with cling film, puncture the top and cook on HIGH for 10 minutes. Turn the potatoes over halfway through.
2 Meanwhile, arrange the onion slices in a layer over the base of a shallow casserole dish. Arrange a layer of carrot slices over, cover with slices of celery and dot with butter. Add 3 tablespoons water.
3 Cover with cling film, puncture the top and cook on HIGH for 8 minutes. Leave to STAND.
4 Arrange the cauliflower florets in a ring around the top of the dish over the celery. Fill the centre with the mushrooms. Season. Pour over sauce mixed with cheese. Cover and cook on HIGH for 10 minutes.
5 Peel the potatoes, mash to a purée with butter and milk and season.
6 Pipe or spoon the purée over the top of the dish, cover with cling film, puncture top and cook on HIGH for 10 minutes. STAND 3-5 minutes.

Vegetable kebabs

Makes 6

12 button onions, peeled and trimmed
½ red pepper, cored, deseeded and cut
into 2.5 cm/1 inch slices.
½ green pepper, cored, deseeded and cut
into 2.5 cm/1 inch slices
2 tablespoons olive oil
2 medium courgettes, cut into 1 cm/
½ inch slices
100 g/4 oz frozen whole mushrooms
3 medium tomatoes, quartered
50 g/2 oz Cheddar cheese, grated
salt and pepper

1 Thread the button onions on to 6 wooden skewers (satay sticks are ideal). Divide the pepper slices between the skewers and place them on a rectangular plate with the vegetables arranged 'top to toe'. Brush the kebabs with a little oil.
2 Cover with cling film, puncture the top and cook on HIGH for 3 minutes.
3 Thread the courgette pieces on to the skewers and brush them with oil. Re-cover, puncture the cling film and cook on HIGH for 1 minute.
4 Trim the mushroom caps level with the stalks and thread the caps on to the skewers. Add tomato quarters to each skewer, brush again with oil and sprinkle grated cheese over all the vegetables. Season well and cook, uncovered, on HIGH for 2 minutes, until the vegetables are cooked and all the cheese has melted.

Variations
When in season, cherry tomatoes are excellent candidates for kebabs.

SAUCES

Sweet and savoury sauces are always successful when made in the microwave cooker and will be thick and creamy every time. Usually the ingredients can first be blended together and then cooked in the serving bowl or jug, cutting down washing-up. Use a container that will allow enough room for the sauce to boil up. Sauces can be reheated very quickly in the microwave and they taste as though they have just been made, so it is a good idea to make and freeze quantities of Basic white sauce and defrost, heat and flavour as required.

Basic white sauce

Makes 300 ml/½ pint
300 ml/½ pint milk
15 g/½ oz frozen sliced onion, or ½ small
  onion, sliced
15 g/½ oz frozen sliced carrots, or ½
  carrot, sliced
a few celery slices
pinch of ground cloves or nutmeg
25 g/1 oz butter or margarine
25 g/1 oz plain flour
salt and pepper

1 Place the milk in a large jug or a bowl with the onion, carrot, celery and spice. Cook on HIGH for 3 minutes, or until the milk comes to the boil. Set aside, covered, for 5-10 minutes for the flavours to infuse.
2 Place the butter in a medium bowl and cook on HIGH for 1 minute 10 seconds until melted. Stir in the flour and mix to a smooth paste.
3 Gradually strain in the flavoured milk and stir until smooth. Cook on HIGH for 2½-3 minutes, stirring after each minute, until thickened and smooth. Season to taste before serving.

Hollandaise sauce

Serves 2-3
2 tablespoons white wine vinegar
1 tablespoon water
100 g/4 oz butter, cubed
2 egg yolks
salt and pepper

1 Heat the vinegar with the water on HIGH for 2 minutes. Stir in the cubed butter and beat well.
2 Add the egg yolks and whisk until combined, then heat on LOW for 15-20 seconds *only*. Whisk in the salt and pepper to taste and cook on LOW for 1 minute or until the sauce thickens.
3 STAND for 1-2 minutes before serving with fish, potatoes or green vegetables such as broccoli or asparagus.

Note: this is a tricky sauce, but the secret is to cook on LOW after adding the egg yolks and watch it carefully. If allowed to boil, the sauce will curdle.

From left to right: Hollandaise sauce, Basic white sauce, Quick jam sauce, Chocolate fudge sauce.

Custard sauce

For desserts and puddings
Makes 600 ml/1 pint
2 tablespoons custard powder or cornflour
1 teaspoon vanilla essence (optional)
1-2 tablespoons caster sugar
600 ml/1 pint milk
7 g/¼ oz butter

1 Place the custard powder or cornflour in a large bowl with the vanilla essence, if used, and the sugar. Blend in the milk gradually.
2 Cook, uncovered, on HIGH for 4-5 minutes, stirring after each minute, until thick. Beat in the butter.

Quick jam sauce

For desserts and puddings
Makes about 300 ml/½ pint
225 g/8 oz raspberry jam
7-8 tablespoons water
1½ tablespoons cornflour
a few drops of lemon juice

1 Place the jam in a large bowl with half the water. Cook on HIGH for 1 minute.

2 Stir the cornflour into the rest of the water and stir it into the jam. Cook on HIGH for 1 minute. Stir well then cook on HIGH for 1 minute.
3 Stir well, add lemon juice to taste and strain, if necessary, before serving.

Chocolate fudge sauce

For ice cream
Makes about 600 ml/1 pint
350 g/12 oz icing sugar
50 g/2 oz cocoa powder
50 g/2 oz cornflour
250 ml/8 fl oz milk .
100 g/4 oz butter, cubed
1 teaspoon vanilla essence
50 g/2 oz chopped walnuts or walnut pieces

1 Mix the icing sugar with the cocoa powder and cornflour in a large bowl. Add the milk and the butter. Do not stir.
2 Cook, uncovered, on HIGH for 4 minutes, then STAND for 30 seconds. Beat in the vanilla and stir in the nuts. Serve hot.

CAKES
AND DESSERTS

The traditional British 'steamed pudding' is only one of the desserts that cooks to perfection in minutes rather than hours when cooked in a microwave. Cakes simply rise up before your eyes – heavy sponges become a thing of the past.

Because cakes are cooked partly by the steam produced in the mixture they can tend to dry out if overcooked – so time the cooking period carefully. The recipe for Orange and almond sponge includes ground almonds which help to keep the sponge moist with their high fat content.

Use flavourings cautiously as the microwave brings out the flavour.

Both shortcrust and suet pastry microwave well. But as neither of them will brown it is wise to use wholewheat flour to make the dish appetizing.

Wholemeal apple and orange flan

Serves 6
For the sweet pastry
250 g/8 oz wholemeal flour
a pinch of salt
125 g/4 oz butter
25 g/1 oz caster sugar
50 g/2 oz ground hazelnuts
8 teaspoons water
For the filling
500 g/1 lb frozen apple slices
75 g/3 oz soft dark brown sugar
2 teaspoons lemon juice
25 g/1 oz butter
3 small oranges, peeled and sliced
1 large orange, thinly sliced and cut in half
For the topping
50 g/2 oz demerara sugar

1 First make the pastry case: place the flour and salt in a bowl. Rub in the butter until the mixture resembles breadcrumbs. Stir in the sugar and hazelnuts and just enough water to make a firm dough.

2 Roll out on to a lightly floured board and use to line a 20 cm/ 8 inch round glass pie dish. Cover the pastry with greaseproof paper, then weight with a similar dish.

3 Cook on HIGH for 5 minutes, then remove the top dish and the paper and cook for 2-3 minutes on HIGH. Allow to cool in the dish.

4 For the filling: place the apples, sugar, juice and butter in a large bowl. Cover with cling film and cook on HIGH for 6 minutes. Drain off and reserve the excess liquid.

5 Beat the apple mixture until smooth, spoon it into the cooled pastry case and smooth the top.

6 Arrange the small orange slices evenly over the flan. Arrange the halved large slices in an over-lapping fan design, working from the edge to the centre. Spoon some of the reserved liquid over the top.

7 Cook on HIGH for 5 minutes, then sprinkle the top with demerara sugar and place under a pre-heated moderate grill for up to 5 minutes until the sugar caramelizes slightly.

Coffee banana ring

Serves 6-8
Makes one 20 cm/8 inch ring cake
125 g/4 oz soft (tub) margarine
125 g/4 oz caster sugar
125 g/4 oz self-raising flour
2 eggs
1-2 tablespoons instant coffee granules
2-3 teaspoons boiling water
1 large banana, mashed
For the Butterscotch sauce
100 g/4 oz butter
5 tablespoons soft brown sugar
5 tablespoons golden syrup
1 tablespoon lemon juice
To decorate
1 banana peeled, thinly sliced and dipped
in lemon juice

1 Place the margarine in a bowl with the sugar, flour and eggs. Dissolve the coffee in the boiling water and add to the bowl with the mashed banana. Beat until smooth.
2 Spoon into a 1.75 litre/3 pint ring mould, smooth top and cover with film. Cook on HIGH for 5 minutes.
3 Remove, lift off film and cover with a plate. STAND for 5 minutes.
4 Place sauce ingredients in a jug. Cook on HIGH 1½ minutes. Stir.
5 Return to microwave and cook on HIGH for a further 2-3 minutes, stirring. Pour evenly over cake.
6 Arrange the banana around cake.

Wholewheat scones

Makes a 21 cm/8½ inch round
100 g/4 oz self-raising flour
pinch of salt
100 g/4 oz wholemeal flour
50 g/2 oz butter
2 tablespoons golden syrup
85 ml/3 fl oz milk

1 Sift the self-raising flour into a bowl with the salt, then stir in the wholemeal flour.
2 Rub in the butter until the mixture resembles fine breadcrumbs. Mix the golden syrup into the milk and gradually add to the flour mixture to make a soft, but not sticky, dough.
3 Knead lightly on a floured board, then roll out into a 21 cm/8½ inch round. Line a ceramic flan dish or a shallow pie plate with cling film and place the dough in the dish. Pat to fit, then mark into eighths with a sharp knife.
4 Cook on HIGH for 4½ minutes.
5 STAND in the dish for 5 minutes. Serve with butter and jam.

Peanut delights

Makes 12
50 g/2 oz soft (tub) margarine
50 g/2 oz soft brown sugar
75 g/3 oz crunchy peanut butter
50 g/2 oz plain flour
¼ teaspoon salt
¼ teaspoon bicarbonate of soda
1 egg, beaten
½ teaspoon vanilla essence

1 Cream together the margarine, sugar and the peanut butter. Sift half the flour with the salt and bicarbonate and stir into mixture.
2 Stir the egg into the mixture, then flavour with vanilla. Add remaining flour and mix to a soft dough.
3 Line a 20 cm/8 inch round dish or container with cling film and spoon in the dough, smoothing the top.
4 Cook on HIGH for 4 minutes, turning the container round halfway through. STAND for 2-3 minutes. Cut into triangles.

Rich chocolate cake

Makes one 25 cm/10 inch loaf cake
125 g/4 oz golden syrup
125 g/4 oz soft dark brown sugar
125 g/4 oz butter
175 g/6 oz self-raising flour
½ teaspoon ground cinnamon
50 g/2 oz cocoa powder
1 egg, beaten
150 ml/¼ pint milk
For the topping
125 g/4 oz plain chocolate
To decorate (optional)
double cream and crystallized violets

1 Grease the inside and the base of a 25 cm/10 inch loaf dish and line the base with buttered greaseproof paper.
2 Place the syrup in a large bowl with the sugar and butter. Cook on HIGH for 2 minutes until melted. Stir.
3 Sift the flour, cinnamon and cocoa together into the bowl, then add the egg and milk and mix thoroughly.

4 Turn into the prepared dish, level the top and cook on HIGH for 5 minutes. Test the centre with a cocktail stick or a skewer. When cooked the skewer will come out clean. Leave to STAND for 5 minutes.
5 Turn out on to a wire rack and cool.
6 For the topping: break the chocolate into a bowl and cook on HIGH for 30 seconds. Stir. Cook for a further 30 seconds until melted and smooth. Spread over the cake and decorate the top, when cooled, with whipped cream and some crystallized violets.

Note: if topping with just chocolate, store the cake in an airtight tin. If it goes a little dry, serve as a dessert cake with softly whipped cream, or split and sandwich with apricot or red fruit jam and a little whipped cream or chocolate buttercream. Decorate with some coarsely grated chocolate or stud with chocolate coffee beans.

Rich chocolate cake (left) and Rhubarb and ginger pudding.

Rhubarb and ginger pudding

Serves 4
50 g/2 oz soft (tub) margarine
50 g/2 oz caster sugar
1 egg, beaten
1 ½ teaspoons ground ginger
100 g/4 oz self-raising flour
3-4 tablespoons milk
225 g/8 oz frozen rhubarb
25 g/1 oz brown sugar

1 Beat together the margarine, caster sugar, egg, ground ginger and flour until smooth. Add the milk.
2 Mix the frozen rhubarb with the brown sugar and place in the bottom of a greased 900 ml/1 ½ pint pudding basin. Put the sponge mixture on top and smooth.
3 Cover with cling film, puncture the top and cook on LOW for 7-9 minutes or until the top of the pudding is firm but still slightly moist and a skewer comes out clean. STAND for 5 minutes.

Orange and almond sponge cake

Makes one 18 cm/7 inch layer cake
175 g/6 oz soft (tub) margarine
125 g/4 oz self-raising flour
50 g/2 oz ground almonds
1 teaspoon baking powder
175 g/6 oz caster sugar
3 eggs
finely grated rind of 1 orange
2 tablespoons fresh orange juice
toasted almonds, to decorate
For the orange buttercream
125 g/4 oz butter, softened
225 g/8 oz icing sugar, sifted
grated rind and juice of 1 orange

Orange and almond sponge cake.

1 Grease the base and sides of an 18 cm/7 inch diameter undecorated soufflé dish and line the base with greased greaseproof paper.
2 Put all the ingredients into a bowl and beat until smooth.
3 Pour the mixture into the prepared soufflé dish and cook, uncovered, on HIGH for 6 minutes. Test near the centre with a skewer.
4 STAND for 10 minutes in the dish before turning out.
5 To make the orange buttercream, beat together the butter, sugar, orange rind and juice.
6 Split and sandwich the cake with some of the buttercream. Decorate with more buttercream and toasted almonds.

Variations
For a plain sponge, substitute 2 tablespoons milk for the orange juice and omit the orange rind. Add a few drops of vanilla essence.

▊ Cherry coffee pudding

Serves 4

2 teaspoons instant coffee granules
2 tablespoons milk
50 g/2 oz soft (tub) margarine
50 g/2 oz caster sugar, or to taste
1 egg
50 g/2 oz self-raising flour
50 g/2 oz glacé cherries, quartered

1 Mix together the coffee granules and milk in a large bowl.
2 Add the margarine, sugar and egg and all but 1 teaspoon of the flour, and beat well until smooth, with a soft, dropping consistency.
3 Toss the quartered cherries in the 1 teaspoon of flour and stir them into the mixture. Grease the base and sides of a 600 ml/1 pint pudding basin and line the base with greased greaseproof paper.
4 Pour the mixture into the prepared basin and cook, uncovered, on HIGH for 5 minutes, or until a skewer inserted into the centre comes out clean.
5 STAND for 5 minutes before serving with a Custard sauce (page 59), or softly whipped cream flavoured with coffee, rum, or both.

Variations
For rum and raisin pudding, flavour with rum or rum essence instead of coffee and substitute 75 g/3 oz sultanas or raisins for the cherries.
For a golden pudding, put 2 tablespoons golden syrup into the prepared bowl before mixing and adding the unflavoured pudding ingredients. Add ½ teaspoon vanilla essence instead of the coffee and omit the cherries. Serve with custard or extra syrup, heated.

▊ Old-fashioned treacle tart

Serves 6

1 (20 cm/8 inch) wheatmeal or wholemeal pastry case (see Wholemeal apple and orange flan, page 60)
For the filling
125 g/4 oz butter
4 tablespoons golden syrup
1 tablespoon black treacle
½ teaspoon vanilla essence
½-1 teaspoon finely grated lemon rind
1 tablespoon lemon juice
125 g/4 oz fresh wholemeal breadcrumbs
1 egg, beaten
To decorate
142 ml/5 fl oz carton double cream
½ teaspoon finely grated lemon rind

1 Place the pastry case on a non-metallic serving dish.
2 For the filling: place the butter in a bowl with the golden syrup, treacle, vanilla essence, lemon rind and juice. Cook on HIGH for 3 minutes, until the butter is melted. Stir well.
3 Stir in the breadcrumbs mixed with the egg and pour the filling into the pastry case. Smooth over the top and cook on HIGH for 4 minutes, turning the plate halfway through the cooking time. Remove from the cooker and allow to cool.
4 To decorate: whip the cream until just stiff enough to hold its shape and with a piping bag fitted with a large star nozzle, pipe 6 large rosettes around the edge. Sprinkle each with a little grated lemon rind and serve.

Variation
Use pastry trimmings, re-rolled and cut into strips to make a lattice top.

Mandarin upside-down pudding

Serves 4-6

125 g/4 oz butter or margarine
100 g/4 oz caster sugar
2 eggs
50 g/2 oz desiccated coconut (optional)
100 g/4 oz self-raising flour, sifted
For the topping
25 g/1 oz butter, diced
25 g/1 oz soft brown sugar
319 g/11 oz can mandarin oranges,
  drained

1　Grease the base and sides of an 18 cm/7 inch diameter soufflé dish.
2　For the topping: dot the butter over the base of the soufflé dish and sprinkle with the sugar in an even layer. Cook on HIGH for 1 minute 10 seconds until melted and combined. Arrange the orange pieces in a decorative pattern in the melted sugar, reserving a few pieces for decoration. Set aside.
3　Soften the butter or margarine on DEFROST for several seconds, then beat with the caster sugar until light and fluffy. Beat in the eggs, stir in the coconut, if using, then fold in the flour.
4　Spoon the mixture over the topping and cook on HIGH for 7 minutes. STAND for 3 minutes before turning out and serving decorated with the reserved mandarin segments.

Variations
For a peach and cinnamon pudding, substitute canned peach halves for the mandarin oranges, arranging a whole almond in the centre of each. Flavour the pudding mixture with ½-1 teaspoon of cinnamon or mixed spice.

For a pineapple and ginger pudding, substitute canned pineapple rings for the mandarin oranges and place a walnut in the centre of each. Flavour the pudding mixture with 1-2 teaspoons ground ginger.
For a cherry-chocolate pudding, use frozen stoned cherries, defrosted, or drained canned ones. Omit the coconut, and add 50 g/2 oz cocoa powder to the mixture, melt 50 g/2 oz dessert chocolate with 1 teaspoon water on HIGH for 2 minutes, then stir into the cake mixture.

Baked egg custard

Serves 4-6

600 ml/1 pint milk
4 eggs, beaten and strained
40 g/1½ oz caster sugar
2-3 drops vanilla essence
a sprinkling of ground nutmeg

1　Pour the milk into a large jug or glass bowl and cook on HIGH for 3 minutes.
2　Slowly whisk in the strained eggs, the sugar and the vanilla essence. Sprinkle a little nutmeg over the top.
3　Cover with cling film and cook on DEFROST for 15-17 minutes. STAND until set. Serve with sponge fingers or poached fruit.

Note: take care not to overcook or the custard may curdle.

Variations
Flavour with the grated rind of half a lemon instead of the vanilla essence and use cinnamon instead of the nutmeg.

MICROWAVE MENUS

SUMMER BUFFET FOR SIX

Savoury vol-au-vents

Poached salmon trout

Summer fruit cheesecake

Savoury vol-au-vents

Fills 12
12 frozen vol-au-vent cases, cooked
For the basic filling
300 ml/½ pint thick white sauce (see Basic white sauce, page 58) made with 75 g/ 3 oz plain flour and 75 g/3 oz butter
For the mushroom filling
15 g/½ oz butter
50 g/2 oz frozen mushrooms, defrosted and finely chopped
25 g/1 oz fennel, chopped (optional)
parsley to decorate
For the ham and asparagus filling
15 g/½ oz butter
75 g/3 oz frozen asparagus tips or the same quantity of canned asparagus, drained
15 g/½ oz finely chopped onion
25 g/2 oz sliced cooked ham, finely diced

1 Make the basic filling. Divide it between two mixing bowls. Set aside.

2 For the mushroom filling: place the butter in a bowl and cook on HIGH for 30 seconds until melted. Stir in mushrooms and fennel, if used, and cook on HIGH for 2 minutes. Stir into sauce in one bowl. Set aside.

3 For the ham and asparagus filling: place the butter in a bowl and cook on HIGH for 30 seconds until melted. Reserve six asparagus tips. Chop remainder. When butter has melted, stir in the onion, ham and chopped asparagus and cook on HIGH for 2 minutes. Stir into the second bowl of sauce. Set aside.

4 Spoon each of the fillings into six pastry cases and replace the tops. Warm for 2 minutes on HIGH, before serving. Garnish the mushroom vol-au-vents with small sprigs of parsley and the others with the reserved asparagus tips.

Poached salmon trout

Serves 6
1 (1 kg/2 lb) frozen salmon trout or salmon, defrosted
To garnish
1 small lettuce, shredded
1 lemon, sliced
¼ cucumber, sliced
1 stuffed olive
To serve
Hollandaise sauce (page 58) or mayonnaise

1 Wipe the salmon and cut the tail fin into an inverted 'V' to neaten.

2 Cover a large plate with cling film and put the salmon trout on the plate.

3 Cover with cling film, puncture the top and cook on HIGH for 12 minutes, turning the fish over halfway through the cooking time.

4 Leave to STAND for 5-6 minutes. Allow to cool completely if serving cold.

5 Carefully lift the skin from the fish with the point of a knife at the head end and peel it off towards the tail. Lay the fish on a bed of shredded lettuce and decorate with slices of cucumber and lemon.

Savoury vol au vents (bottom), Poached salmon trout (centre) and Summer fruit cheesecake (page 68).

6 Place half an olive over the eye. Serve with a green salad and accompany with Hollandaise sauce or mayonnaise.

Variations

For a flavoured mayonnaise: divide 600 ml/1 pint mayonnaise into three portions. Flavour one with tomato purée and a dash of Tabasco sauce, a second with orange or lemon juice and sprinkle the third with 1 tablespoon of chopped spring onion.

Summer fruit cheesecake

For the base
175 g/6 oz ginger biscuits
50 g/2 oz butter
For the topping
225 g/8 oz cottage cheese
225 g/8 oz full-fat cream cheese
142 ml/5 fl oz carton natural yoghurt
50 g/2 oz cornflour
grated rind and juice of one lemon
50 g/2 oz sultanas
175 g/6 oz caster sugar
2 eggs, beaten
To decorate
fresh kiwi fruit, peeled and sliced
frozen or fresh raspberries

1 Grease the base and sides of a
   900 ml/1½ pint soufflé dish and
   line with cling film. Finely crush the
   biscuits and place them in a bowl
   with the butter. Cook on HIGH for
   1 minute, then mix the biscuits and
   butter together. Spread this over
   the base of the soufflé dish and
   press it down well.
2 Press the cottage cheese through a
   fine sieve. Mix with the cream
   cheese and yoghurt to form a
   smooth mixture, then beat in the
   cornflour. Stir in the lemon rind and
   juice, the sultanas and sugar. Beat
   in the eggs and pour the mixture
   over the base.
3 Cover the top of the dish with cling
   film and cook on DEFROST for
   20 minutes. Leave to STAND for
   10 minutes and if the centre of the
   cheesecake has not set, cook on
   DEFROST for a further 5 minutes.
4 When cooled, decorate the top of
   the cheesecake with slices of kiwi
   fruit and raspberries. Chill briefly
   before serving.

**SUPPER
FOR FOUR**

**Asparagus with two
butters**

**Spicy pork and
prawn pilaf**

Hot fruit salad

Asparagus with two butters

Serves 4
*750 g/1½ lb frozen asparagus or fresh
  asparagus, trimmed*
For lemon butter
75 g/3 oz butter
2 teaspoons lemon juice
1 teaspoon grated lemon rind
1 tablespoon chopped parsley
salt and pepper
For orange butter
75 g/3 oz butter
1 tablespoon orange juice
1 teaspoon lemon juice

1 For lemon butter: place the butter
   in a jug and cook on DEFROST until
   softened slightly. Beat in the lemon
   juice and rind, parsley and season.
   Shape into a 2.5 cm/1 inch roll,
   wrap in foil and chill.
2 Arrange the asparagus in a shallow
   dish tips inwards. Add 2-3
   tablespoons water. Cover with film,
   puncture the top and cook on HIGH
   for 7 minutes. Rearrange, cover again
   and cook on HIGH for 7-8 minutes.
   STAND, covered, for 5 minutes.

3 For orange butter: place butter in a jug with the orange juice and the lemon juice and cook on HIGH for 2½ minutes until melted. Check the flavour and seasoning, adding a little extra orange juice if necessary.

4 Serve the hot asparagus on individual plates, topped with thin slices of chilled lemon butter. Serve the hot orange butter separately.

Spicy pork and prawn pilaf

Serves 4-6
225 g/8 oz easy-cook long grain rice
300 ml/½ pint boiling water
300 ml/½ pint dry white wine
1 tablespoon oil
¼ teaspoon turmeric
¼ teaspoon paprika
¼ teaspoon ground coriander
¼ teaspoon ground ginger
6 cloves
¼ teaspoon ground cumin
6 cardamom pods, lightly crushed
25 g/1 oz pine nuts or flaked almonds
1 teaspoon salt
100 g/4 oz frozen petits pois
50 g/2 oz frozen mixed diced peppers
100 g/4 oz frozen sliced mushrooms
2 tablespoons oil
500 g/1 lb frozen pork tenderloin fillet, defrosted and cubed
100 g/4 oz frozen peeled prawns
salt and black pepper

1 Place the rice in a bowl and set aside. Combine the water and wine and cook on HIGH for 3 minutes, or until boiling. Pour this over the rice with the oil, spices, pine nuts or almonds and salt. Cover with film and cook on HIGH for 10 minutes. STAND, covered, for 10 minutes.

2 Put the peas in a separate bowl with the peppers and mushrooms. Cover, puncture the top and cook on HIGH for 2½ minutes. Stir, re-cover and cook on HIGH for a further 2½ minutes. Drain and stir into the rice.

3 Heat the oil in a large, shallow dish for 1 minute on HIGH. Add the pork and cook for 4 minutes on HIGH, stirring halfway through cooking. Add the prawns, and season with salt and pepper. Cover with film, puncture and cook on HIGH for 4 minutes, stirring once.

4 Add the pork and prawns to the rice. Toss all the ingredients well to combine and reheat on HIGH for 1-2 minutes before serving.

Hot fruit salad

Serves 4
350 g/12 oz mixed dried fruit, such as apples, pears, apricots or prunes
150 ml/¼ pint water
300 ml/½ pint dry white wine
25 g/1 oz soft brown sugar, or to taste
¼ teaspoon ground cinnamon
¼ teaspoon allspice, or mixed spice
1 tablespoon brandy or dry sherry
To serve
150 ml/¼ pint double cream

1 Place the dried fruit in a large bowl and pour in the water and wine. Cover with cling film, puncture and cook on HIGH for 5 minutes.

2 Stir in the sugar, cinnamon, allspice or mixed spice and the brandy or sherry. Cover and cook on HIGH for 7 minutes.

3 Leave to STAND, still covered, for about 30 minutes, until the fruit is plump and tender.

4 Serve hot with whipped cream.

CHRISTMAS LUNCH

Roast turkey
Traditional trimmings
Christmas pudding

Roast turkey

*1 (4.5-5.5 kg/10-12 lb) frozen, self-basting
  turkey, defrosted
500 g/1 lb frozen pork sausagemeat,
  defrosted
1 large onion, peeled
salt and pepper*

1 Stuff the breast cavity of the turkey with the sausagemeat. Fold down the flap of skin and secure in place with wooden skewers or cocktail sticks, or by tucking the flap underneath the wing tips.
2 Place the onion inside the body cavity. Season with salt and pepper and tuck the ends of the legs into the top of the vent. Tie round with string to keep them in place.
3 Set the turkey, breast-side up, on a large flan dish the same size as the turntable, or on a microwave roasting rack. Cook on HIGH for 35 minutes.
4 Take out bird, cover loosely with foil and STAND for 35 minutes. Drain and reserve excess cooking juices for basting and/or gravy.
5 Cover the bird loosely with a slit roasting bag and set, breast-side up again, on the dish or rack to finish cooking on HIGH for a further 35 minutes.

6 Remove from the cooker, discard the roasting bag and pour off the rest of the juices. Remove the onion. STAND for 35 minutes, covered tightly with foil.
7 Pierce the thickest part of the thigh with a skewer. If the juices run clear, the turkey is cooked. If not, remove the foil, and cook turkey for 5 more minutes. Test again. It should now be ready to serve.

Turkey giblet gravy

*giblets from the frozen turkey, defrosted
600 ml/1 pint water
1 tablespoon cornflour
a few drops of gravy browning (optional)
salt and pepper*

1 Place the giblets in a dish and pour over the water. Cover, bring to the boil on HIGH, then cook on DEFROST or SIMMER for 15 minutes.
2 Remove the giblets. Blend the cornflour with 150 ml/¼ pint of the giblet stock and add a few drops of gravy browning, if a darker gravy is preferred.
3 Bring the rest of the stock to the boil on HIGH, stir in the cornflour mixture and cook on HIGH for 2 minutes, stirring once, until thickened.
4 Season, cool rapidly, cover and store in the refrigerator, unless using immediately. (Add some of the cooking juices from the turkey when reheating to serve.)

Roast turkey trimmed with Bacon-sausage rolls and Buttered parsnips, Cranberry-orange sauce, Bread sauce, Creamed potatoes, Brussels spouts with almonds; Christmas pudding with Brandy Butter.

Buttered parsnips

Serves 4-6
3 tablespoons water
salt
750 g/1½ lb frozen parsnips, peeled and
*   quartered*
25 g/1 oz butter
freshly ground black pepper

1 Pour the water into a wide, shallow
  bowl, add a little salt and arrange
  the parsnips in a single layer, if
  possible. Cover with cling film,
  puncture the top and cook on HIGH
  for 12 minutes until tender. Stir
  them about halfway through the
  cooking time.
2 STAND for 5 minutes, then toss in
  the butter and season generously
  with freshly ground black pepper.

Brussels sprouts with almonds

Serves 4-6
500 g/1 lb frozen Brussels sprouts
salt and pepper
25 g/1 oz flaked almonds, toasted in the
*   microwave cooker (see page 16)*

1 Cook the sprouts from frozen (in a
  dish) for 12 minutes on HIGH.
2 STAND for 5 minutes, drain, then
  season and scatter over the almonds.

Bread sauce

Makes 300 ml/½ pint
1 onion, peeled
6 cloves
75 g/3 oz fresh white breadcrumbs
50 g/2 oz butter, cubed
salt and pepper
300 ml/½ pint milk

1 Stud the cloves around the onion
  and place it in a bowl. Add the
  breadcrumbs, butter and seasoning
  and pour over the milk.
2 Cover with cling film, puncture the
  top and cook on HIGH for 5
  minutes.
3 STAND, covered, for 15 minutes,
  then take out the onion. Thin the
  sauce down with a little extra milk,
  if necessary.
4 Cook, uncovered, on HIGH for
  2 minutes, stirring once during
  cooking. Stir again and adjust
  seasoning to serve.

Cranberry-orange sauce

100 g/4 oz caster sugar
175 g/6 oz fresh or frozen cranberries
grated rind of 1 orange
3 tablespoons orange juice
a few drops of lemon juice

1 Place the sugar in a bowl with the
  cranberries, orange rind and juice.
  Cover with cling film and cook on
  HIGH for 4 minutes. Add lemon
  juice, to taste.
2 Stir well, cover again and cook on
  DEFROST for 10 minutes, stirring
  once during cooking.
3 Purée and chill the sauce before
  serving.

Bacon-sausage rolls

Makes 12
350 g/12 oz frozen pork sausagemeat,
*   defrosted*
12 streaky bacon rashers, rinds removed
*   and stretched with the blade of a knife*

1 Divide the sausagemeat into 12 portions, then roll each one into a small sausage shape. Wrap each in a rasher of bacon, securing with a wooden cocktail stick, if necessary. Arrange on absorbent kitchen paper in a shallow dish.

2 Cook on HIGH for 10 minutes. Test. Cook 1-2 minutes more, if necessary.

Creamed potatoes

Serves 6

1 kg/2 lb potatoes, peeled and cut into even-sized pieces
3 tablespoons water
150 ml/¼ pint hot milk
25 g/1 oz butter
salt and pepper

1 Place the potatoes and water in a bowl and cover with cling film. Puncture the top and cook on HIGH for 17-20 minutes. STAND for 5 minutes.

2 Add the milk, butter and salt and pepper, mash together until smooth.

Christmas pudding

Serves 4-6

75 g/3 oz plain flour
a pinch of nutmeg
a pinch of mixed spice
75 g/3 oz butter, softened
175 g/6 oz raisins
100 g/4 oz sultanas
100 g/4 oz currants
25 g/1 oz flaked almonds
75 g/3 oz soft dark brown sugar
2 eggs, beaten
grated rind of 1 orange
grated rind and juice of 1 lemon
2 tablespoons black treacle
1-2 tablespoons brandy
a little gravy browning (optional)

1 Sift together the flour, nutmeg and mixed spice. Beat in the softened butter, add the dried fruit, almonds and sugar and mix in the eggs.

2 Stir in the orange rind, lemon rind and juice and the black treacle. Add brandy to taste and a little gravy browning, if a darker mixture is preferred.
DO NOT ADD THE TRADITIONAL METAL COINS TO THE MIXTURE.

3 Grease the inside of a 1.2 litre/ 2 pint pudding basin and pour in the pudding mixture. Cover with greased greaseproof paper or cling film and secure with string, or an elastic band.

4 Cook on HIGH for 10 minutes. Let STAND for 10 minutes, then turn out the pudding. Cover loosely with cling film. When cold, wrap in greaseproof paper and foil and store in an airtight container.

Note: the pudding keeps well for up to 2 months. To reheat, cover with clingfilm, place on a serving plate and cook on HIGH, allowing about 1 minute per 450 g/1 lb. STAND for 1 minute. Serve with brandy butter or rum sauce.

Brandy butter

Serves 4-6

100 g/4 oz unsalted butter
100 g/4 oz caster sugar or icing sugar
3 tablespoons brandy

1 Place the butter in a bowl and cook on DEFROST until softened.

2 Add the sugar and beat until the mixture is pale and creamy. Add the brandy a little at a time, until flavoured to taste.

3 Chill well before serving.

73

PRESERVES

Making jams and chutneys in the microwave means that you won't be spending the whole day in the kitchen stirring a hot bubbling preserving pan full of fruit or vegetables. Most preserves can be made in under one hour, leaving you and the kitchen cool – a boon in summer months.

The fruit and vegetables used will not only keep their colour when cooked in the microwave but will retain their shape and more of their natural texture and their full flavour.

Don't confine yourself to using only fruits and vegetables that are in season – frozen fruits and vegetables make delicious preserves and the Three-fruit marmalade, for example, can be made at any time of the year.

▌ Three-fruit marmalade

Makes 1 kg/2 lb
1 grapefruit
3 medium oranges
1 lemon
700 g/1½ lb granulated sugar

1 Pare the rind from the fruits and shred very thinly.
2 Halve the fruits and squeeze out all the juice into a large bowl. Scrape out and roughly chop the flesh.
3 Add the chopped flesh and rind to the juice with 225 g/8 oz of the sugar. Cover with cling film and cook on HIGH for 8 minutes.
4 Stir in the remaining sugar, cover and cook on HIGH for a further 10 minutes. STAND for 5 minutes.
5 Spoon a little marmalade on to a chilled saucer and allow to cool. Test for setting – it will wrinkle when pushed with a fingertip. If not, return to the cooker and cook for 1 minute intervals until it does.
6 Pour into warm sterilized jars. When cool, cover, seal and label.

▌ Peach conserve

Makes about 1 kg/2 lb
500 g/1 lb peaches
2 tablespoons lemon juice
350 g/12 oz granulated or caster sugar

1 Halve, stone and roughly chop the peaches. Place in a large bowl with the lemon juice, cover with cling film, puncture the top and cook on HIGH for 6 minutes. Remove covering and stir in the sugar.
2 Place, uncovered, in the microwave and cook for about 20 minutes on HIGH, stirring during the first few minutes to ensure that the sugar is dissolved. Continue cooking until setting point is reached (see recipe for Three-fruit marmalade).
3 Carefully fill warmed sterilized jars with the jam and allow to cool. Cover, seal and label.

Variations
Add ¼ teaspoon cinnamon for a spicy peach conserve. Use apricots instead of peaches.

Sweet piccalilli

Makes about 1.5 kg/3 lb
225 g/8 oz aubergines, chopped
225 g/8 oz frozen cauliflower florets
225 g/8 oz frozen diced mixed peppers
225 g/8 oz frozen sliced courgettes
100 g/4 oz frozen onion slices
175 g/6 oz salt
1.5 litres/2½ pints water
75 g/3 oz sugar
2 teaspoons dry English mustard
½ teaspoon ground ginger
450 ml/¾ pint white vinegar
2 tablespoons plain flour
1 teaspoon turmeric

1 Place the vegetables in a large bowl. Dissolve the salt in the water and pour over them. Leave for 24 hours.
2 Next day, drain and rinse thoroughly in cold water. Drain well.
3 Blend the sugar with the mustard, ginger and 300 ml/½ pint of the vinegar in a large bowl. Add the vegetables and mix well. Cover with cling film, puncture top and cook on HIGH for 15 minutes.
4 Blend the flour and turmeric with the remaining vinegar and stir into the mixture. Cook, uncovered, on HIGH for a further 5 minutes.
5 Carefully fill warmed sterilized jars.

Simple apple chutney

Makes about 1.5 kg/3 lb
700 g/1½ lb frozen apple slices
500 g/1 lb frozen onion slices
175 g/6 oz soft brown sugar
300 ml/½ pint wine vinegar
grated rind and juice of 1 lemon
100 g/4 oz sultanas
salt
a pinch of cayenne pepper (optional)
8 whole cloves

1 Place the apples in a large bowl with the onions and sugar. Pour on half the vinegar, then cover with cling film, puncture the top and cook on HIGH for 6 minutes.
2 Stir in the lemon rind and juice, the sultanas and the rest of the vinegar. Season with a little salt and add cayenne, if liked, and the cloves.
3 Cook, uncovered, on HIGH for 10 minutes, then stir well. Cover and cook on HIGH for 10 minutes, then stir again. Cook, uncovered, on HIGH for 10 minutes.
4 STAND until cool, then pour into sterilized jars, cover and seal.

From left to right: Three-fruit marmalade, Peach conserve, Simple apple chutney and Sweet piccalilli.

SUPPERS
AND SNACKS

Ideas to suit all occasions, from pasta and rice dishes to the omelettes and creamy scrambled eggs that the microwave cooks so well. There are fillings for everyone's favourite baked potato, spicy devilled kidneys – and some of the dishes can double as first courses for more formal meals. Though the time-saving is not great for pasta and rice, the results are excellent and there are no messy saucepans. The accompanying sauces can be quickly put together during standing time required for most dishes.

Omelette

Serves 1
15 g/½ oz butter
2 eggs, beaten
3 tablespoons milk
salt and pepper
chopped parsley (optional)
grated parmesan (optional)
To garnish
tomato halves and watercress sprigs
* (optional)*

1 Place the butter in a 20 cm/8 inch shallow flan dish or pie plate and cook on HIGH for 30 seconds until melted and the fat coats the base evenly.
2 Beat the 3 tablespoons milk into the eggs and season with salt and pepper. Cook on MEDIUM for 2½-3 minutes, stirring the sides towards the centre two or three times to ensure even cooking.
3 Fold the omelette over in the dish and sprinkle with chopped parsley, or sprinkle with grated Parmesan and finish under a pre-heated hot grill for a few seconds. Serve garnished with the watercress and tomatoes, if using.

Kedgeree

Serves 4
225 g/8 oz easy-cook long-grain rice
600 ml/1 pint boiling water
1 tablespoon oil
1 teaspoon salt
750 g/1½ lb frozen smoked haddock
* fillets, defrosted*
50 g/2 oz butter, diced
2 hard-boiled eggs, chopped
100 g/4 oz frozen sweetcorn
pepper
2 tablespoons single cream or top milk

1 For the rice: place the rice in a bowl and pour on the boiling water. Stir in the oil and salt. Cover and cook on HIGH for 10 minutes. STAND, covered, for 7 minutes.
2 Place the haddock in a shallow dish. Cover with cling film and cook on HIGH for 3½ minutes, then turn the fish over and continue to cook on HIGH for 3½ minutes. Drain and flake the fish, removing any skin.
3 Stir the fish into the rice with the butter, eggs and corn. Season.
4 Cover and cook for 4 minutes, stirring once. STAND for 2 minutes, stir in cream or milk and serve.

Bacon savouries

Makes 12
4 streaky bacon rashers, rinds removed
and cut into three
12 cooked prunes, stoned

1 Wrap a piece of bacon round each prune and secure with a wooden cocktail stick.
2 Arrange around the edge of a large plate lined with absorbent kitchen paper. Cover with a piece of kitchen paper and cook on HIGH for 2 minutes. Turn each roll upside down and cook on HIGH for 3 minutes, or until the bacon is cooked. Serve with mustard, pickle or a fruit relish.

Brewer's snack

Serves 1 or 2
2 slices wholemeal bread
For the topping
100 g/4 oz mature Cheddar cheese,
grated
2 tablespoons chopped, sliced cooked
ham
25 g/1 oz butter
¼ teaspoon mustard powder
1 tablespoon brown ale or beer
salt and pepper

1 Make the toast under a conventional grill and set aside to keep warm.
2 Mix together the topping ingredients and season to taste. Place the mixture in a large bowl and cook on HIGH for 30 seconds. Stir well and continue to cook on HIGH for 30 seconds, or until bubbling.
3 Pour over the toast and serve.

Supper-snack scrambled eggs

Serves 4
4 large eggs
salt and pepper
1 tablespoon milk
25 g/1 oz butter
To serve
4 slices hot buttered toast

1 Break the eggs into a large jug and beat well with a little salt and pepper and the milk.
2 Add the butter and cook on HIGH for 3 minutes, stirring after each minute, until the desired consistency is reached. Serve on hot buttered slices of toast.

Variations
For Scotch woodcock, use only the yolks of the eggs and cream instead of milk, and spread the toast with anchovy paste.
For Golden eggs, beat in 1 teaspoon chopped fresh tarragon, or ¼ teaspoon dried tarragon with the eggs. With the butter, add 100 g/4 oz frozen smoked haddock fillet, skinned, defrosted and flaked into small pieces.
For Salmon eggs, add 100 g/4 oz frozen smoked salmon, skinned if necessary, defrosted and chopped instead of the haddock.
For Corn eggs, add 25 g/1 oz frozen sweetcorn, with the butter and substitute 1 tablespoon chopped fresh chives or parsley for the tarragon.
For Asparagus eggs (a delicious dinner party starter), chop and add 4 or 5 frozen asparagus tips, defrosted, then chopped. Substitute chives for the tarragon.

3 Heat the butter for 1 minute on HIGH. Add the ham and mushrooms and cook for 1 minute on HIGH.
4 Drain the pasta and stir in the ham and mushroom mixture. Add the cream and toss to mix. Sprinkle with cheese and toss to mix, then sprinkle generously with black pepper to serve.

Note: the pasta should be covered completely by the water so the exact quantity depends on the container. Wide, shallow dishes are ideal.

Spaghetti alfredo.

▌ Spaghetti alfredo

Serves 2
1.25 litres/2 pints boiling water (see note)
1 teaspoon salt
1 tablespoon oil
225 g/8 oz short spaghetti, or flat noodles
100 g/4 oz butter, cubed
100 g/4 oz ham, diced
50 g/2 oz frozen sliced mushrooms
150 ml/¼ pint double cream
75 g/3 oz grated Parmesan cheese
black pepper

1 Pour the boiling water into a large bowl or a wide, shallow dish. Add the salt and the oil. Carefully add the spaghetti, making sure it is all under water. If not, cook uncovered on HIGH for 1 minute, then push the rest under.
2 Cover and cook on HIGH for 5 minutes. Stir, re-cover and cook on HIGH for 5 minutes. STAND, covered, for 10 minutes.

▌ Devilled kidneys

Serves 3
8 frozen lambs' kidneys, defrosted, membranes and cores removed
25 g/1 oz butter or margarine
1 small onion, finely chopped
1 tablespoon dry sherry
1 tablespoon Worcestershire sauce
¼ teaspoon mustard
1 tablespoon chopped parsley, to garnish

1 Slice the kidneys and set aside.
2 Place the butter in a shallow dish and cook on HIGH for 40 seconds until melted. Stir in the onion, cover with cling film and cook on HIGH for 2 minutes. Stir, then cook on HIGH for 1 minute.
3 Add the sliced kidneys, cover and cook on HIGH for 2 minutes. Stir, cover and cook on HIGH for 2 minutes. Add the sherry, Worcestershire sauce and mustard. Stir, cover and cook on HIGH for 2 minutes, then STAND for 3-5 minutes.
4 Sprinkle with parsley and serve with plain toast.

Baked jacket potatoes

Serves 4
*4 potatoes, each weighing about
225 g/8 oz*

1 Wash and dry the potatoes and
 prick the skins in several places.
2 Arrange the potatoes, well spaced,
 on absorbent kitchen paper and
 cook on HIGH for 10 minutes.
3 Turn the potatoes and cook on
 HIGH for a further 10 minutes.
 STAND for 5 minutes.

Jacket potato fillings

1 **Ploughman's potato**: split cooked
 potato, sprinkle with 2 tablespoons
 Cheddar cheese. Serve with dark
 pickle and garnish with parsley.
2 **Farmer's potato**: cook 1 chopped
 bacon rasher on HIGH for 2
 minutes. Add 4 slices Continental
 sausage, cooked, and 2 sliced
 prunes. Split potato and arrange
 filling inside. Serve with mustard.
3 **Fisherman's potato**: heat 2
 tablespoons defrosted cooked
 prawns in 25 g/1 oz butter on HIGH
 for 2 minutes. Beat shrimps into 2
 tablespoons cream cheese, fill the
 split potato and sprinkle with a
 pinch of cayenne.
4 **Hunter's potato**: melt 10 g/¼ oz
 butter on HIGH for 30 seconds.
 Add 4 button mushrooms and
 50 g/2 oz chicken liver, sliced.
 Cover and cook for 2 minutes on
 MEDIUM. Fill the split potato.
 Season well and serve with
 watercress.

*Baked jacket potatoes, from the top:
Hunter's potato, Farmer's potato,
Ploughman's potato and Fisherman's
potato.*

INDEX

ACKNOWLEDGEMENTS
Photographer: Laurie Evans
Stylist: Sue Russell
Home economist: Judy Bugg